Self-Publishing Empire™ Book #1

Entity Set Up

Why and How Authors
Need to Create a Business Entity Now

Michael L. Banner

ISBN: 1-947510-07-X
ISBN-13: 978-1-947510-07-4

Published by

www.toesinthewaterpublishing.com

Why Do You Need <u>This</u> Book...

<u>This</u> Whole Series Of Books?

Do you agree/identify with any one of these author quotes?

"I love writing, but I hate the business side of self-publishing!"

✓"I don't mind self-publishing, but I want my books to look like they've come from a traditional publisher."

✗ "I want to take on a co-author but don't know how to set-up the logistics."

✗ "If I die, I want to easily pass my book royalties on to my family."

✗ "I can't do it all myself: I need a partner to help me with my self-publishing business."

"I'm worried about protecting my books and author name from being copied or stolen."

"I'm doing well, but I'm worried about taxes and maybe even liability."

"I'd like to know more ways to supplement my writing income by leveraging my brands, without working much more than I am now."

"I want to build my publishing business up to unimaginably big levels!"

I'm guessing if you're reading this, you agreed with one or more of these.

No matter what your needs are as an author, if they concern the business side of self-publishing, *Self-Publishing Empire*™ was written for YOU!

But why <u>This</u> Series of Books?

There are hundreds of fine books already out there on the mechanics of self-publishing your book, the craft of writing, advertising on Amazon (and other mediums), how to set up newsletters, how best to explode readership, writing really-really fast, and so on. But search Amazon and you'll have difficulty finding many (if any) books which teach self-publishers:

> - How to easily run the business side of your writing business; and
> - how to pass on your book royalties to your family members, so that what you've created produces income long after you're gone; and
> - how to co-author with somebody, so that the business logistics are set up and managed properly; and
> - how you protect your self-publishing business against liability; and
> - how to use the new tax laws to minimize your business taxes; and
> - how to take on a partner, while protecting yourself; and
> - how to protect your author and/or title brands from piracy and theft; and
> - how to increase your business income, over and above what your own writing can provide, without working much harder; and
> - how to grow your self-publishing business to levels which would make even traditional publishing

companies envious.

In other words... How to build a Self-Publishing Empire™.

The fact is, there is very little written about the actual business mechanics of setting up and running a self-publishing business as an INC or LLC, taking on partners and growing your publishing income stream so that you and your family have sustainable income now, as well as long after you're gone.

The concepts discussed in this series don't have the sex appeal of writing 5000 words in an hour, or how to magically sell billions of books in one day if you follow some as-yet untried secret formula. But the concepts discussed in this series of books are as important as those juicier-sounding topics—more so, if you really want to develop a sustainable self-publishing business.

And this is why I started writing *Self-Publishing Empire™*.

What is the *"Self-Publishing Empire™* series of books?

I initially sat down to write one book called *Self-Publishing Empire™* to help authors with all of the mundane but absolutely necessary tasks of creating and running an author entity, just as I had done for myself.

But as I spoke with other authors about this book's concepts, I heard a need for more info than what I had planned to cover. So I decided to "kick it up a notch," as one famous chef used to say. *Self-Publishing Empire™* has now evolved from hundreds of discussions with self-published authors across the globe who seemed puzzled by and wanted more information about the complexities of protecting their intellectual property, how to leverage their brands into more earnings, ways to minimize their taxes, and the mechanics of taking on other author-partners and/or co-authors—in other words, how to grow their self-publishing businesses larger than what even they could have imagined.

UPDATE: So, you might ask, why a series of books instead of one large book?

Too much for one book - As I hinted, there was so much material going into this book, and this project was taking far longer than I had hoped. So I decided to break it up into more bite-sized books, some of which (like this one) I wanted to release right away.

And there was another big reason why...

The Trademark - When I filed for a trademark on "Self-Publishing Empire" (I will describe this in more detail in book #3 in the series, *Protecting Your IP*), I had only one book planned. Then I found out I needed to publish at least one more book to prove the brand. You see, a title of one book is not a brand in itself, no matter how popular it is. Therefore it's not trademarkable. But a title of a series, on two or more books, is a brand and therefore is trademarkable.

For these two reasons, and a few others, I decided to release *Self-Publishing Empire*™ as series of seven (or more) books.

> ⚠ **FREEBIE ALERT**: There are multiple forms, agreements and contracts discussed in this book. The text of a couple is listed in the book. However most forms, including the fillable forms, are available to you for download for free. Just give me your name and email and I'll send you a password to access the forms database on selfpublishingempire.com. **See "Forms" in the Appendix for details.**

For more details on what's included in the rest of the series, go to *What's in This Book*.

STOP!

Just to put your mind at ease, *Self-Publishing Empire™* is NOT some way for me to generate speaking fees, or to cross-sell you into some expensive training seminar or workshop: I do NOT have an online course that I'll ask you to buy at the end of this book. This series of books is all I will produce on this subject. PERIOD! *Self-Publishing Empire™* is my way of giving back to a community which has helped me so much.

Don't get me wrong, I am still charging you a fair price for these books, to compensate me for my time and knowledge on these subjects. But that's it. I'm too committed to running my own self-publishing businesses, working with our co-authors, and of course, writing my own novels.

In other words, these books are all I plan to offer on these subjects.

So soak up as much as you can.

What do I know? Who am I?

I'm the author of eleven sci-fi novels (under the pen name M.L. Banner), which have sold over 100,000 copies in my short five years of writing (as of 5/1/19). I've won awards, still manage my own catalog of books, and continue to write more books. I have four books planned for release—in addition to the *Self-Publishing Empire™* series—this year. I write because I absolutely fricking love it. But I also enjoy the business side of self-publishing too... I know that makes me a bit of a weirdo in most self-publishing circles.

But you have to understand, I'm what is called a serial entrepreneur (someone who regularly starts new businesses). I've enjoyed this stuff so much that I've sat on the boards (still do) of other start-ups and consulted thousands of small biz owners over the years on how to set up their enterprises and manage their business affairs. I have even created a company that helps others start their own businesses. SmallBiZ.com, Inc., a business filing services company, is now twenty years old and has formed, filed, and assisted with over 100,000 small business corporations or LLCs. Still, my absolute favorite businesses are my self-publishing enterprises, and that is why I'm involved in several.

I'm telling you all of this not to boast, but to point out that I have come to intimately know the mechanics of setting up and running a business long before I self-published my first book and then chose to build my own Self-Publishing Empire™.

Now, let me help you build yours.

My goal for you

My goal is to give you many of the tools you'll need to create your own Self-Publishing Empire™, whether that means forming a simple partnership between you and a co-author, or writing just a few books, or taking up writing as a full-time career, or even growing... no, EXPLODING your author business into something huge.

In a nutshell...

> The *Self-Publishing Empire™* series will give you a complete game plan, literally everything you need to help you set up and run your publishing enterprise: creating your author entity (INC or LLC) and matriculating with the IRS, your state, and various vendor platforms like Amazon; managing your entity properly, after it has been created; setting up multiple streams of income;

recruiting other authors to your enterprise and setting up co-authoring arrangements, without spending thousands in attorney fees; protecting your brands and other intellectual property; minimizing your taxes and having your publishing company pay for your vacations, completely tax free; and finally, perpetuating your family legacy, so that what you've created lasts longer than you do.

I'll show you how to do all of this yourself or, if you don't want to DIY any part of this, how to use professionals to help you do it all for you.

Still not convinced?

What if I told you that the government will reimburse you for all the costs to set up your Self-Publishing Empire™, including your author entity and then some?

NOW that I have your attention...

2018/2019 Tax Changes

The IRS wants you to set up your Self-Publishing Empire™

You may not know this, but the federal government now wants you to form a business entity for your Self-Publishing Empire™ (for simplicity I'm going to say SPE), and the new tax law proves it!

The 2018 Tax Cuts & Jobs Act, which officially took effect 1/1/2018, has made the need to create a new pass-through entity (i.e., S Corporation or LLC) almost absolutely necessary, especially in the field of self-publishing. And even though this law has been in effect since January 1, 2018, the IRS and tax professionals have been working through how to apply this new law on business and personal tax payers throughout 2018. In fact, it was only on 01/18/2019, over one year after the law was passed, that the IRS released its final ruling on how businesses are to be treated when it comes to the biggest and newest deduction... Section 199A.

NOTE: For details on how your SPE will deal with some of the most important tax issues, see *What Authors Need to Know About Taxes (Self-Publishing Empire Book #7)*. However, I'll give you the juiciest benefit to come out of the new tax law.

The 20% Pass Through Deduction

As of 1/1/2018, any taxpayer owning and running a business through a pass-through entity will receive **a 20% deduction on all net "qualified business" income for individuals with individual incomes up to $157,500 ($315,000 for joint filers)**.

In other words, before you apply your federal tax rate against your net (after deductions) royalty income, you'll get to reduce it by 20%!

Let's do some math

Assume you're going to make net royalty income of $50,000 in 2018. That's net of your regular business expenses. In the past, you would pay taxes on that $50,000 at your current individual tax rate. As of 1/1/18, the federal government allows you a deduction on that income, if you collect your royalty income through a "pass-through entity."

Let's see what that looks like:

The New Pass-Through Tax Benefit

	Without a Pass-Through Entity	With a Pass-Through Entity
Royalty Income	$50,000	$50,000
20% Deduction	(0)	(10,000)
Taxable Income	$50,000	$40,000
Federal Tax*	$4,370	$3,170
Tax Savings		**$1,200**

* Federal Tax assumes a single person, with no dependents, and no other income, using the Standard Deduction.

Did you get that?

The IRS, through the newest tax rules, is going to pay you $1,200 (in this example) to collect your royalty income through your new entity! Why wouldn't you take them up on it?

Preferred Businesses

This $157,500 personal income ($315,000 for joint)

threshold only applies to certain businesses which the IRS considers not preferred. Now here's the GREAT news: SELF-PUBLISHING IS ONE OF THOSE "QUALIFIED" BUSINESSES! And that means if your SPE is run through a pass-through entity, whether your SPE's income is really high or very low, you'll receive the maximized benefit not only for last year, but in future years.

What's a "Pass-Through Entity"?

For the purposes of our discussion about the new IRS regulations, a "pass-through entity" includes a partnership, a sole proprietorship (AKA an Individual who solely owns a business), an S Corporation business entity, and in some cases trusts and estates.

Notice, I didn't mention a Limited Liability Company (AKA: LLC). But in fact...

The IRS Prefers LLCs

There are a whole host of other benefits (see below and *Section II: What REALLY is an Author Entity*) for forming a new LLC, but the new tax law now makes it obvious that your SPE should be owned and operated by an LLC.

I'll dive into the details later in the book, but whether you expect to make very little or a lot of money with your self-publishing empire, the way the new tax rules are set, your best tax advantages are with forming an LLC.

Other Tax Benefits of a Business Entity

You'll receive many more benefits just for running your SPE through a business entity, and more specifically an LLC. Here are a few:

> **Write off your vacation** - You can deduct the cost of your next vacation (from your net income), thus reducing your taxable income even more. I know this sounds like a bad plot line, but wait until you hear how to do this.

> **Reduce Self-Employment Taxes** - If you pay self-employment taxes on your income now (you probably do), your LLC can elect instead to pay you a smaller (but reasonable) salary, and the balance of your income isn't subject to S.E. Taxes.

> **Buy other books for research** - More than just this book, and other "How To" self-publishing or business books, you can deduct the next big romance novel from you business income. To be a good writer, you must read. So reading other books, by other writers, even not in your genre is an acceptable business expense. From now on, have your publishing company pay for your reading habit. I do.

> **Deduct your Prime, KU and other subscriptions** - Do you have legit business reasons to subscribe to these and other services? If it benefits your business, you betcha! Yes, I know you might also check out the latest cooking show video and then download a cookbook while planning your next holiday meal, but that's beside the point.

Read about these and other benefits in *What Authors Need to Know About Taxes (Self-Publishing Empire Book #7)*.

Check out what else is in this book...

What's In <u>this</u> Book

Here's what you can expect to find in this book

Book Layout

Some of the subjects covered in this book (and others in the series) are complex. To simplify, I use the following Icons to highlight an important topic:

 Check Points - A list of points, displayed this way, rather than a large block of text, to make it easier to read.

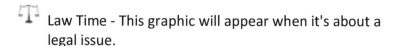 Law Time - This graphic will appear when it's about a legal issue.

 "Yield" Symbol - When you really need slow down and pay attention.

 Hot Idea - When there's something cool I want to point out to you.

In general, I've done my best to make this book as readable as possible, as well as usable as a reference, all the while you continually grow your writing and self-publishing business into a Self-Publishing Empire™.

Reading order

Jump around and read any of the juicy parts first (if you want), before diving into the more complex or mundane. Yawn! However, like a good character arc, this book is laid out in the order I would suggest you read it. And if that's too much to ask, and you come to a part you just can't bear—because it feels like a day in the dentist chair—I give you this...

Quick Read

You <u>need</u> to get back to writing your next best-seller and not spend too much time reading about how to set up your Self-Publishing Empire™. Plus, I acknowledge there are some dry bits within, no matter how much I try to dress them up with humor. That's why at the beginning of each Section, I've written a Quick Read—think Cliff Notes. That is, I'll explain in as few words as possible all the important stuff that I am covering in more detail in each of the chapters of that section.

Outline of the Book

I. Why Authors <u>NEED</u> an entity, NOW!
- o Quick Read
1. Tax Savings
2. Your Publisher Image
3. Partnerships
4. Transferability
5. Liability Protection (In General)
6. Defeat Sole Prop-ism
7. Your Corporate History
8. Future Changes Harder to Make
9. Instant Credibility
10. Unexpected Liability
11. Unexpected Death/Disability
12. Co-Author Partnerships
13. Segment Projects
14. Privacy
- o Why Wrap Up

II. What <u>REALLY</u> is an Author Entity?
- o Quick Read
1. What is a Sole Proprietorship?
2. What is a Corporation?

3. What is an LLC?
4. What is Corporate Personhood?
5. Which Entity Type is Best For you?

III. Prepare to Form YOU Publishing, LLC
○ Quick Read
1. Why is Your Entity Name So Important?
2. Choosing a Formation State
3. Get Help or DIY?
4. Filing Worksheet - LLC
5. Entity FAQs
6. Step by Step

IV. Immediately After: What You Must Do!
1. Next Steps For Your LLC
2. Next Steps For INCs
3. Agreements & Contracts
4. Getting a Tax ID

V. Introducing YOU Publishing LLC
1. Setting Up Your Bank Accounts
2. Credit Cards and Credit Lines
3. Registering With Publishing Platforms
4. Communications & Getting Social
5. Are YOU Done Yet?

What comes next?

APPENDIX
1. 51 State Agencies & Their Processes
2. Agreements
3. Free Incorporation Coupon

What's covered in other books of the *Self-Publishing Empire™ Series*

Book #2: Managing Your Author Entity

After your entity is set up, you're not done. Ongoing actions must take place to keep your entity legally compliant and up to date. I will make it simple.

1. Internal Actions & Documentation
2. LLC Management
3. INC Management
4. What to Do with the State
5. What to Do with the IRS

Book #3: Protecting An Author's Intellectual Property
You have multiple brands, but what are you doing about protecting them? Find out the pitfalls of doing nothing (with real case studies) and how you can easily and inexpensively protect all your brands.

1. What are your Empire's brands?
2. How Do You Protect Them?
3. Copyright Protection
4. Amazon Just Took Down My Books For Trademark Infringement
5. Cockygate Revisited
6. Trademark Protection
7. Vigorous Defense of Your IP

Book #4: Multiple Streams of Income
Your SPE is making money. Now it's time to leverage your brands and create multiple streams of income

1. Become a Hybrid
2. Put Your Books on Auto-Pilot
3. More Formats
4. Co-Author/Partner
5. Box Sets
6. Affiliate Revenues (Amazon & Others)
7. SWAG for Sale
8. Podcasts
9. Becoming a Publisher of Other Books
10. License your World

Book #5: Co-Authoring and Author Partnering

This has become a popular practice, and perhaps you have done this already with another author... But was it done right?

1. Questions You and Your "Partner" Should Ask Each Other
2. Define Roles
3. How to Divide the Income?
4. The Business Side of Things - Whose Account or a New One; Which Bank
5. Writing Agreements
6. How to Set Up a Separate LLC for Your Partnership
7. Contracts

Book #6: Author Legacy

What happens after you are gone? How do you plan for this?

1. Why This Is Important
2. Review of What's Been Done (Which Helps Your Legacy Planning)
3. Plan for Succession
4. Next Steps Now

Bonus ADVANCED STUFF

1. Income Splitting
2. Separate Ownership of Each Book/Series

Book #7: What Authors Need to Know About Taxes

Including more details on the most recent tax rules and how they affect your author business.

1. Tax Basics for Businesses
2. The Tax Cuts and Jobs Act
3. Self-Employment Taxes & S-Corps
4. Reporting to IRS & Your State
5. The Power of an Accountant/CPA
6. Year-End Stuff

Bonus: WRITE OFF YOUR NEXT VACATION - The fun stuff

1. Making Your Vacation Tax-Free
2. Why Not Do Research on that Vacation
3. Writers' Conferences
4. Prime & KU Subscriptions
5. Other Books

A Quick Commercial

Before we dive in, I wanted to give a quick word about SmallBiZ Filings (currently on Smallbiz.com). This is the company that I created almost twenty years ago to help small biz owners, like you and me, to set up their new corporation or LLC inexpensively, quickly and professionally.

So here's my pitch...

Yep, you read that correctly.

As a purchaser of this book, I'm going to have SmallBiZ.com set up one INC or LLC for you for free. In other words, SmallBiZ.com will waive its normally low $25 fee to form your Self-Publishing Empire™ (either as an INC or LLC) just for you. You'll pay only your state's filing fees (as little as $50, depending on the state in which you reside or want to form in) and a small shipping and handling fee ($6 for Standard Shipping).

Why am I doing this?

To help introduce this company to you. That's because, besides setting up your publishing INC or LLC, SmallBiZ.com offers other services and products for your corporation or LLC. My hope is that you'll use one of them as well. I'm also doing this to promote this book and get *Self-Publishing Empire*™ books into the hands of as many self-published authors as possible.

To get your coupon for your free INC or LLC and to read the terms and conditions of this offer, go to the book's Appendix.

But first, ask yourself...

Are You A Real Business...

Or is self-publishing just a hobby?

Authors are notorious for shorting themselves when it comes to their self-publishing businesses. They focus on their writing, which makes sense. But when it comes to investing money into their businesses, they are either completely unwilling or had never planned to do so... until <u>after</u> they have made money, often stating, "I can't afford to do so at this moment."

Is that you?

Before we even talk about setting up and then building your Self-Publishing Empire™, please <u>really</u> consider whether or not you intend to operate a real business.

In other words... Is your writing a hobby?

A hobby is something that you do for fun, when you have the time, and you don't really expect to make money from it. Therefore, you don't intend to spend a lot of money on your hobby, unless you can justify it... or you win the lottery.

Is self-publishing a hobby for you? Or is it a true business, like any other enterprise where you recognize that it will require a proper investment of your time and money to make it successful? Or do you look at this as the type of activity where, if it makes a profit at some point, you might consider reinvesting some of the proceeds back into it? Perhaps you're thinking when you're making enough money from your writing to live off the net royalties, then on <u>that</u> day, you'll be all in?

I know, we've all read about those writers who launched their self-publishing businesses with their first book, all done on the cheap, and somehow, miraculously they've reaped tens of thousands of dollars (or more). And once they did, they became serious about their own Self-Publishing Empire™. Hugh Howey and Amanda Hawking are names that come to mind. This has become the goal of many self-published authors.

I'm sorry to tell you, those days are mostly gone.

⚠ If you plan to make money with your self-publishing, especially enough to live on and write full-time, you'll need to treat your writing as a business from the very beginning: You'll need to invest a substantial amount of time and some money right away to make sure it is successful later.

But if you're not at this point right now, understand that your writing <u>is</u> a hobby that maybe <u>wants</u>

to become a business.

This is perfectly fine. However, you probably don't need this book... Yet.

Is your writing a business?

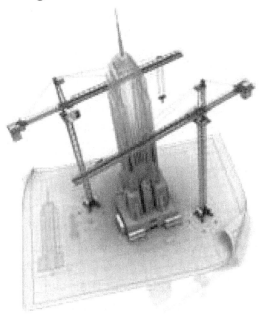

Starting and managing a business is something that requires a specific investment of time and money before you can even hope to make a substantial profit, much less make a living from it. You might get lucky, but that's not your plan. You are planning for the long haul: to build your business until some point in the future, when it will become profitable, and maybe even your full-time vocation.

Not sure you want to invest money into it?

Tell me if this make business sense: You start a business where you design a product in a highly competitive marketplace, but you decide at the start NOT to take any time to research your prospective customers (you're just going to build the product you want), you choose the cheapest materials for your product and you don't care how professional the manufacturer was or what your product looks like (you just don't have the money to make it better), you're going to set up a Facebook page as your only means for customer contact and sales, and you don't plan on spending any money on marketing?

Would you really expect this business to be successful and sell millions of its products?

Of course not.

So why, then, do so many self-published writers take the following path with each book they produce:
> they write only the book they want, irrespective of their readers;
> they use DIY covers;
> they don't hire professional editors, proofreaders and formatters;
> they don't set up a professional author website; and
> they don't invest any money in the marketing of their books.

And yet, somehow, they expect to sell millions of copies, but they're surprised that only a couple of copies were bought, most likely by their immediate family.

Time to get serious

Treat your writing business like the business empire that you want to build. From your brand to the products you produce, you need to look at your writing as a business.

If you've decided you are a business (and not a hobby) and you're all in from this moment forward, what do you say... Let's start your Self-Publishing Empire™!

How Far Do You Want to Take this?

Little self-publisher or giant publishing house - it's your choice!

Bob Williams loves the French wine country and is intimate with every part of it, from his work for different wineries to knowing the people of that area. He turned those loves into a best-seller about the lives of the people within a fictional wine community. After a few more books, Bob is ready to take the plunge, leave his employment, and follow his goal... to write more of what he loves, while making a living doing it full-time.

Jay J. Falconer is a successful entrepreneur, computer programmer and avid sci-fi fan. He took some time and fulfilled a lifelong dream of turning some of his ideas into a two-book series. But they barely sold. He knew he was missing something and focused on the business end of self-publishing, turning out two more series of books, selling over 100,000 copies. He has since gone on to form a publishing house with an author friend (yours truly), with the intent of becoming a leader in its genre. He'd still like to write more books and screenplays, but later. Now his desire is to use what he and his partner have learned to help other authors become best-sellers.

How far do you want to take your author business?

The great thing about the *Self-Publishing Empire™* concept is that no matter how small or how huge you want to become as a self-publisher, you can use this series of books to create your own "empire," in your own way. In other words, the model works no matter what your goals look like.

The fact is, most writers don't want to do anything more than write; the business details are often the boring part and are therefore ignored. But I want you to consider, as the owner/manager of your own Self-Publishing Empire™, what you can achieve is boundless, if you want. And if you don't want such lofty goals, that's fine too.

But first you have to make a decision.

Where do you want to invest your time?

© Toon In The Water Publishing LLC

As with every decision, whatever your goal is for your SPE, it comes down to where you are willing to commit your time. If all you want to do is write a couple of books a year, because that's all you want to do and you want to make a living off that, but you have no interest in going any further, your time commitment is different than if you wanted to build your publishing business to the point where you'll take on other authors to write for you, personally expanding your brands globally, and more.

What if you could have your cake and eat it too?

Best of Both Worlds

Even if you are like Boo, in that your only goal is to write books full time, if you're self-publishing, you'll still need to commit some time to the business side of things. But your focus is different than the self-publisher who wants to grow huge.

Your focus is going to be on making a living, while still growing your business so as to protect your income in the event something happens to you and you stop writing, even if that's not by choice.

The good news is if you follow what this book advocates, it may mean an initial diversion of some of your writing time (invested into the business side of things), but the benefit to you and your family will be the financial freedom to do as much or as little writing as you want.

Follow me as I give you *Entity Set-Up: Why and How Authors Need to Create a Business Entity Now (Self-Publishing Empire Book #1)*.

Empire

1. "a large commercial organization owned or controlled by one person or group."

2. "an extensive operation or sphere of activity controlled by one person or group."

~ Dictionary.com

Self-Publishing Empire™

1. an author entity created by you to own and manage all of your writing-related income, and possibly much more.

2. get ready; you're about to create one!

Ch I.

Why Authors <u>NEED</u> an INC (or LLC) <u>NOW</u>!
It's more than just protection!

If you had a child, you would nurture your child, make sure your child was strong and able to take care of himself or herself, and then you would send your child off on their own, as their own person, ready to take on the world.

Your author enterprise is much like this. The big difference is that I am recommending that you kick your child out of the house now, long before it's even close to reaching maturity!

"What the heck are you talking about?" you might ask.

Your publishing business is your "baby." Tax and legal

professionals have often argued that you should wait to incorporate (i.e., form a corporation or LLC on behalf of) your self-publishing "baby" only <u>after</u> it has "grown up" (i.e., matured to a point of achieving profitability). Some so-called experts have stated there's no rush in forming an entity, which is analogous to your allowing your progeny to live in your basement, even after becoming an adult—the general idea being that you don't need the protection of forming an entity until after your company is making money, and preferably lots of it.

I say, **"YOU ARE WRONG!"** Kick your progeny out of the house! Now!

In other words, I'm suggesting that you not wait until later, but form your publishing entity now!

Why go from YOU, doing business as "YOU Publishing" to "YOU Publishing LLC"?

There are many reasons for doing this. I'm going to give you fourteen reasons why, as an author, you need to form your entity, and not just some day in the future, but now.

Why Authors Need an INC or LLC NOW

QUICK READ

In the chapters that follow, I cover each of the below points in detail. I recommend that you read each chapter.

It may be unsportsmanlike of me to offer the climax of these chapters ahead of the build-up. But for those of you with A.D.D., like me, what follows is a quick overview of the top fourteen reasons why, as authors, you need to form your entity and not just some day in the future, but now.

The Normal Reasons (to set up):

> **Tax Savings** - With the addition of the new 20% Pass-Through Deduction, setting up an entity almost becomes an

absolute necessity for authors. The details are truly complicated and best left for your CPA/accountant to untangle. Yet even without these new hugely positive changes, a Corporation or LLC enjoys many more tax benefits over a Sole Proprietorship.

> **Your Publisher Image** - Your image as a self-publisher starts with your publisher name. Which one looks better: *YOU doing business as YOU Publishing* or *YOU Publishing, LLC*? Your publisher's name shows up on each book description. And this "image" extends out to your website, FB page, etc. When you are self-publishing and your business is incorporated, it imbues professionalism. In fact, if you take some other recommended steps, your publishing business will look no different, and perhaps even better, than most traditional imprints. In short, if you're serious about setting up a lasting publishing business, you will want to form a business entity.

> **Partnerships** – If your publishing business has two or more partners (i.e., husband and wife), an entity makes everything simpler: vendors, publishing platforms, bookstores, etc. are dealing with one legal entity rather than two individuals.

> **Transferability** - If by some chance you wish to sell your publishing business, this would be much easier if your publishing assets (i.e., your catalog of titles, ISBNs, brands, etc.) are controlled by one business entity.

> **Liability Protection (In General)** - This might not seem like an important issue; after all, what can we as authors hurt except other people's feelings? But liability can come in many forms: charges of copyright or trademark infringement, or perhaps something in the commentary you wrote for your book may be considered malicious and/or libelous, and so much more. By setting up an entity to own and operate your writing business, you are better protecting your <u>personal</u> assets by separating them from your publishing <u>business</u> assets.

Reasons To Set Up Right Now (not later):

> **Your Corporate History** - Your corporate history only starts the day after you have incorporated (or formed an LLC). Unfortunately, some banks, credit issuing vendors, merchants, and others may look down upon your publishing company if it has not been around very long. So why wait? Get incorporated now, and later when your company is very profitable, your corporate history will shine.

> **Future Changes Harder to Make** - Let's assume that you have already set up your publishing accounts, your books on each platform, and even your books' ISBNs all in *your* name (not to mention copyrights, trademarks, etc.). And you continue to do this for every book in the future. Then years later (when the "experts" say you should), you finally form your publishing entity. Imagine then changing everything over to your publishing entity's name (and unique identifier). It is so much easier to do it right away.

> **Defeat Sole Prop-ism** – I made this "ism" up. Yet you have probably experienced this: banks, vendors, review blogs, and so many others often look negatively upon Sole-Prop (Sole Proprietor) self-published authors. This is rarely the case with a corporate publisher (i.e., YOU Publishing, LLC) which of course has signed you on as its primary author.

> **Instant Credibility** – We have already established that your image as a publisher is all important. Taking your publishing company's credibility seriously should not start after your business has achieved profitability; it starts immediately.

> **Unexpected Liability** - Maybe a character in one of your books is exactly like a real person, or you have included an actual person's name, or you have inadvertently used someone else's brand or mark in your work. The point is, you may not know what

you have done until long after you have done it, when someone sues for liability. Trying to create your author entity after this will be too late. You need to form before a liability occurs.

> **Unexpected Death/Disability** – It is too late to try and get something done after you have died or become disabled. With a business entity, especially an LLC, you can easily set up your agreements to give your heirs membership (ownership) in your LLC, before your death. Do it now, while you can.

Other Reasons:

> **Co-Author Partnership** - Say you want to write a new series with another author, or set up a multi-author boxed set, or even co-write just one book with someone else. One of the easiest ways to control and own this type of limited project is to form an LLC and have the LLC own and operate the project. It is easy to set up each of the participants as a member/owner of the LLC, with an equal percentage of ownership/profits (or whatever you agree upon). This LLC would be separate from your own publishing company.

> **Segment Projects** - What if you wanted to write a book or series of books, on a topic you think might cause some public blowback or maybe even extra liability for you? For instance, what if your book shines a very unfavorable light on a particular religion, specific town, private corporation, or political figure? To shield yourself from further liability and scrutiny, and to prevent your other valuable business assets from being hurt by this special project, form a separate LLC to own and run this project. Again, this LLC would be separate from your own publishing company.

> **Privacy** - If you want to branch out into a different genre, you may be considering a new pen name, so as to not confuse or upset the readers in your current genre. But what if you wanted to explore something more sensitive, or racy, or (fill in the blank)? You

could still go with a new pen name, but when you file a copyright, your personal (legal) name will be forever attached to that work, easily findable by anyone who is looking. But if you filed the copyright under your SPE's name... or better yet, under a newly created publishing entity, specifically for that genre, now you have complete privacy. I give a specific example of how that's done in the chapter.

Let us now dive into more details, by looking at each of these reasons independently, including some case studies.

If you feel you have all the reasons you need to form an entity, let me recommend you jump ahead to *Section II: What is an Entity*. You may think you know what an entity is all about, but I guarantee you'll learn a thing or two, which will help you down the road with your own entity.

Ch I. 1.

Reason #1 - Tax Savings

This is the biggie, usually.

Tax savings are also the most common reason why small businesses form a business entity. There is no reason why authors shouldn't take advantage of these same benefits.

There are many federal tax laws that were set up to benefit small businesses, the idea being that if more small businesses are fostered to start and grow (some becoming large businesses), they will create more jobs, all of which increases the tax base. Nowhere is this "favoritism" to business more evident in the federal tax code than with the 2018 Tax Cuts & Jobs Act (the rules of which didn't get finalized until 2019), which provided a huge new tax deduction for owners of "pass-through entities."

Before your eyes roll over into the back of your head, no worries... I'm going to only highlight a few of the top reasons why an entity can help you on the tax side.

> ⚠ Note: Entity tax savings and ways to reduce your taxes will be explored much more thoroughly in **What Authors Need To Know About Taxes (Self-Publishing Empire™ Book #7)**

Your tax adviser can give you more details as well. But here are some of the best:

Pass-Through Entity Deduction - I highlighted this already at the opening of this book. But this one could be a doozie for you! A 20% deduction, off the top of your "Qualified Business Income," which is not subject to federal taxes. And it is only available to pass-through entities, like the author entities we are discussing in this book.

Savings on Self-Employment Taxes - Author entities that have made an "S Election" with the IRS (i.e., filed a document with the IRS) will have their profit or loss *"pass through"* to the entity's owners (and show on a line of their personal tax returns). This means you pay taxes very much like a sole proprietor does, but with one huge exception.

"S Corporations" (an author entity that has made this S Election) can separate their corporate profits from their personal wages. When done right, you as the owner of the "S Corporation" will pay self-employment taxes (Social Security Taxes, and the like) ONLY ON YOUR WAGES, AND NOT ALL OF YOUR PROFITS, as you could potentially with a sole proprietorship.

EXAMPLE: You net $75,000 from your writing. If all of this was paid to your "S Corporation," you could for instance pay yourself $25,000 in wages, on which you would have to pay/withhold employment taxes of 15.3%, or $3825. But now your S Corp. has $50,000 profit left over. Because it is a profit from your

S Corp., you do not have to pay employment taxes on this amount (you would have most likely paid Self-Employment Taxes on all $75,000 as a sole proprietor), which nets you $7,650 in tax savings... ONLY because you had an author entity that elected to take advantage of this one tax benefit.

This one is worth repeating...

> **"Your S Corp... nets you $7,650 in tax savings."**

Easier Separation = More Deductions - It is far easier to separate business from personal when your author entity owns your business assets (read *What is Corporate Personhood?* in the next section for a better explanation of how an entity separates business from personal). This "separation" makes it easier for an entity to pay for something which otherwise might be questionable if it were paid for out of a personal account, and therefore take a business deduction.

The tax law describes a business expense pretty clearly. But there are expenses which are not so black and white, and when paid for by the entity, are less likely to be questioned by the IRS as a personal expense.

Write Off Your Next Vacation - This is one of my favorite examples with the above benefit of "easier separation = more deductions." Again, technically this benefit is available to any sole proprietorship too; it's just easier with an entity. Here's the thinking:

Want to do research for your next book? Why not do it in Tuscany, or Fiji? If you do it right, and your entity pays for everything, 100% of the expenses associated with that trip are deductible against your entity's net income.

This too will also be covered in greater detail in the Bonus Section of *What Authors Need To Know About Taxes (Self-Publishing Empire™ Book #7)*.

Profit Sharing & Retirement Plans - A corporation has the ability to set up one of several profit sharing and/or retirement plans which are not available to the individual sole proprietorship.

These are just a few of the highlights. And again, more detail will be dedicated to each in further volumes.

State Taxes

I'm not going to cover this here, because every state is different, and some have a more negative tax schedule for certain types of entities. The point is, examine all potential state tax issues with your tax adviser before you set up your author entity.

Special Note: Whether you form an entity or not, you'll want to hire a CPA/accountant to help you navigate the complexities of the tax law, which were made much more difficult with the new tax law. A good tax adviser will help you find the best tax savings available to you and your specific situation.

Now onto Reason #2...

Ch I. 2.

Reason #2 - Your Publisher Image

Look like a traditional publisher, or even better!

This is probably an odd #2 for most people, but it is *really* a big reason to create an entity for your writing business.

Your image as a publisher starts with your author entity name. Which one looks better:

YOU, doing business as YOU Publishing

or

YOU Publishing, LLC

Your publisher name (assuming you chose to "imprint" this on your books) shows up on each book description. And this "image" extends out to your website, FB page, etc. When your publishing company is incorporated (again formed as a corporation or as a limited liability company), it imbues professionalism. Anyone who sees this knows that you are serious about your business.

As Good As Or Better Than Traditional

When you look at a book on Amazon, produced by a "traditional" publisher, you see this in Product Details:

Now here's an indie...

Can you tell the difference? There's no publisher listed, and it definitely looks like an indie.

What about this one, in the same sub-genre category: Is it indie or traditional?

Indie! In fact, this one is mine.

Now, you could of course list a publishing DBA here, and you should do that at a minimum. Amazon doesn't require that your publishing name be an entity, and they don't make you prove this. But this is just one step.

Your entity name should also be on your book's copyright page and in its ISBN registration

Add your SPE's brand name (your entity's name) to its own website, Facebook page, email, etc., and your professional image will only be enhanced.

In short, if you're serious about setting up a lasting publishing business, you will want to form a business entity.

Now, check out Reason #3...

Ch I. 3.

Reason #3 - Partnerships

The basic building block to success

Entities like limited liability companies were designed for partnerships.

We will pursue this topic in much more detail in *Co-Authoring & Partnering (Book #6)*. Until then, here are some of the benefits of creating an entity and running a partnership through it rather than just signing a partnership agreement:

- **Publishing platforms prefer it** - You can't set up an account under a partnership's name as easily as you can an entity.

- **Easier for vendors/customers** - They only have to deal with one person (the entity) and not two or more.

- **Better liability protection** - With a general partnership (one born by a written agreement or a handshake), each partner is potentially burdened by the liability caused by the other. And that liability is personal.

- **Better protection** - If you set up an account with a publishing platform, such as Amazon, in your partner's name, the money is theirs. It would be up to you to try and get it through the court system.

- **Partnering with your partner's spouse** – You mean that's not a benefit? Seriously, if your partner dies, his/her spouse and/or beneficiaries might end up being your partner. With an LLC, this can more easily be managed so that it doesn't happen.

It's also another reason why an author entity works so well. Rather than dealing with two people (i.e., two partners), vendors, publishing platforms, bookstores, etc. are dealing with one: YOU Publishing LLC.

Let's go to Reason #4...

Ch I. 4.

Reason #4 - Transferability

How would you sell your publishing business assets?

You may not think it is even a remote possibility right now, but at some point, you may want to sell your self-publishing business.

This might lead you to ask...

Why would I sell?
Here are a few reasons:

1. **Boredom** - Perhaps you are bored with your genre, even though it has made you money, and you want to move into a different genre under a different pen name.

2. **Tired of the business** - Perhaps you want to move away from the business side of things and just write for a publisher.

3. **Retirement** - Nowadays, making money being an author may require a constant schedule of production. Maybe you want to stop producing at such a rate and write only for fun.

4. **Death or Disability** - What if you had no choice: Maybe you have become disabled or you are not here any longer, and your spouse or partner may need to sell?

Even with a big enough backlist and a valuable enough brand, you won't be able to easily sell if all the assets of your publishing business are owned by you personally.

Never happen to me!
Don't think it's possible to sell your self-publishing business? It happens all the time. Just Google "buys indie imprint" or "buys indie publisher" and read all the deals which have occurred in the last five years.

If your backlist is big enough and/or your brands valuable enough, you will undoubtedly catch the eyes of some larger publishers out there. You are starting to sound more like a self-publishing empire already, aren't you?

Again, even with the size and quality of assets, if your author business is not owned by a business entity, you will have little chance of joining the list of indie publishers who have sold.

Think of all the publishing or writing assets you personally own:

- ✔ Books
- ✔ Pen Names
- ✔ ISBNs
- ✔ Copyrights
- ✔ Trademarks
- ✔ Social Media Profiles
- ✔ Websites & Domains
- ✔ Royalties Owed
- ✔ Residuals

Now imagine having to sell each one of these individually, or transferring each and every asset to a new buyer.

It is far simpler and faster to have all of your self-publishing assets owned by one business entity—in other words, your Self-Publishing Empire™. And you have made it easier and faster for a publisher to buy; your Self-Publishing Empire™ instantly becomes more valuable and therefore more marketable.

Get ready, Reason #5 is huge...

Ch I. 5.

Reason #5 – Liability Protection (In General)

Because you're a target!

© SelfPublishingEmpire.com

I know what you are thinking... Are you serious—liability? After all what can we as authors hurt except other people's feelings by our written words?

But liability can come in many forms. Here are just a few:

- **Copyright infringement** - Have you ever posted (on FB or your website) a picture you grabbed from another website or news site? Did you get the copyright holder's permission? What about quoting lyrics in a book? You are guilty of copyright infringement!

- **Trademark infringement** - What if the title to a book

you chose was already trademarked for the same use, and the owner of that trademark has millions of dollars at its disposal for lawyers?

- **Malicious comments** - Have you written commentary about someone who is real or similar to someone real? What if they consider your comments malicious?

Any one of these actions, whether because of your writing a book or posting comments on a website, may cause you to be liable to another for "damages."

Separation = Shield of Protection

By setting up an author entity, which then would own and operate your author business assets, you are separating your personal from your business assets. This is akin to creating a shield of protection for you and your personal assets.

The idea is that if your author entity (not necessarily you) does something which may cause perceived harm, your author entity becomes the primary target, not you and your personal assets.

Now, having this shield of liability doesn't mean that you may not still be still considered personally liable for your actions. But the shield of liability that comes from your author entity is one more layer of protection between you and your personal assets and your business assets.

Now check out Reason #6, which I'll bet you've never considered...

Ch I. 6.

Reason #6 - Defeat Sole Prop-ism

And Self-Pub-ism too!

Yes, I made up the word Sole Prop-ism. Yet you've probably experienced this kind of "ism" before with professional book reviewers, book blogs, and foreign publishers, as well as banks, vendors, and so many others who often look down on upon sole-prop (sole proprietor) self-published authors.

This is not so much the case with a corporate publisher (or imprint), who has a contracted author or authors writing books for them.

NOTE: A brand-new business is always looked down upon, or at least scrutinized more than an established business, regardless of business structure. But having a corporate structure definitely gives your business a leg up over sole proprietorships, at least in the eyes of others.

In other words, YOU Publishing LLC (Your Imprint), represented by its Manager (you!), which has by the way just signed you on as its primary author (YOU Publishing, LLC could have many other authors under contract too, right?), will be less discriminated against than a typical self-published author, when approaching these third parties on his/her own.

Here is another big one: Reason #7...

Ch I. 7.

Reason #7 - Your Corporate History

Don't wait to get it started!

Who is more likely to get a bank loan: a toddler or an adult?

It is no different with a business entity. In other words, younger isn't better when it comes to entities!

When banks or other credit sources (i.e., vendors, credit card companies, merchant companies, etc.) look at your author business entity, they'll be less likely to extend you credit if your entity is brand new than if it has been around for a year or more.

So, taking this logic further, if you wait to form your entity until after everyone says it is time (i.e., when you are extremely profitable), your corporate history has only just been begun. It (not you) will at that point have ZERO corporate history.

Therefore, starting your business entity today rather than later is usually the best way to go. That way, when you might need to show a longer corporate history, you'll have it!

So why wait: Get incorporated now and later, when your company is very profitable, your corporate history will shine that much more.

Reason #8 is huge...

Ch I. 8.

Reason #8 - Future Changes Harder to Make

Do it right the first time!

When is it easier to make a change, now or later?

Once you form your author entity, assuming you are already selling books, you'll need to move all of your business assets from personal ownership to the business, including: your publishing accounts, your books, and even your books' ISBNs, copyrights, trademarks, etc.

All of these must be transferred to your author entity.

Then every subsequent book, copyright, or trademark will be easily set up in your author entity's name.

Imagine if you had to wait to form your business entity when everyone else tells you to, sometime in the future. If years later, you form your author entity, imagine all the work that you would have to go through changing every book's information, not to mention all the other assets, into your author entity's name. Imagine how much more difficult it will be to switch everything; every additional book is that much more work.

It's so much easier to do it right the first time.

Now onto Reason #9...

Ch I. 9.

Reason #9 - Instant Credibility

It starts now!

The moment your author entity is formed, you will instantly gain some new credibility. At a minimum, you will receive some new titles.

As a sole proprietor of your author business, you were just the "owner" or principal, but once you're the owner of your author entity, you are:

- The Manager of YOU Publishing, LLC (if your author entity is a limited liability company) or President of YOU Publishing, Inc. (if your entity is a corporation); and you are

- Editor-in-Chief (of YOU Publishing, LLC); and you are

- Whatever you want to call yourself.

This may not seem like a big deal, but possessing the title of a company, which is an entity, means that you are a serious businessperson. And others will notice.

Isn't it interesting that when a teenager hits eighteen, credit card companies now recognize this person as an adult and a potential spending person and offer them a credit card, even though they have not necessarily shown any creditworthiness? Your author entity is looked at the same way the moment it comes into existence. And because its information is public, you will start to receive all sorts of offers:

- Credit cards
- Credit to buy things (i.e., office supplies, vehicles, and various business services)
- Business loans
- Membership to business groups

Admittedly, once your author entity is formed, you will be the benefactor of a lot of junk mail as well. And your bank might not want to lend your entity money until it is a bit more seasoned (as I mentioned earlier). But don't fret; the rest of the world knows you're somebody now, and everyone will want to do business with you.

And this credibility doesn't start after your author business has achieved profitability or after achieving some other metric; it starts instantly.

But even if the credibility garnered by an author entity is not important to you, protecting your author assets from what comes because of Reason #10 should be...

Ch I. 10.

Reason #10 - Unexpected Liability

Because sometimes things don't go as planned

© SelfPublishingEmpire.com

Maybe a character in one of your books is exactly like a real person, or you inadvertently included an actual person's name in your book, or accidentally used someone else's brand or mark in your work, or your co-author wants a larger share of the pie and threatens to sue...

The point is, you may not know what you have done until long after you have done it and someone sues for libel. And by that time, it will be too late to create your author entity.

There is no way to predict when that moment might come. You are better off creating your author entity now, and not after you need to.

You better plan for Reason #11 as well...

Ch I. 11.

Reason #11 - Unexpected Death/Disability

You will not see it coming!

Setting up an author entity will not save you from all the perils that life throws at you. But having one in force when something happens will make everything easier for you, and even more so for your loved ones, if you suddenly depart this world and go to the great writer's conference in the sky.

I will cover this topic in much more detail in *Author Legacy (Self-Publishing Empire Book #5)*. But here are a few reasons why you'll want an entity set up *before* something happens to you:

- **Give your spouse/partner authority** - If you are the owner of all your author assets and business accounts (i.e., publishing platforms, trademarks, bank accounts, vendor accounts, etc.) then you've made life that much more difficult for your spouse/partner if you die or become disabled. Your spouse/partner, in your absence, would have to prove his/her authority as account holder to take control and, in the event of your death, formally change ownership. However, if your author entity is already the owner, then there is nothing to change: your spouse/partner instantly becomes the manager, but the owner remains.

- **Avoid probate** - A properly set up author entity avoids having a probate court possibly interfere in your author business affairs. This makes the transfer to your spouse/partner that much easier.

- **Ease of transfer** - Because you own your author entity, and your author entity owns all of your author assets, it becomes fairly easy to transfer your ownership interest in the author entity when you want—or in this case, when something unforeseen happens to you.

If some or all of your author assets are co-owned with a partner, the reasons for having an author entity set up ahead of time are doubled:

- **Your partner's spouse is now your partner** - If your partner is the one suddenly taken, your partner's estate's beneficiaries take over your partner's ownership and potentially management of your partnership. That usually means his/her spouse. But if you set this up in your author entity and agreements ahead of time, this can be avoided.

- **How about your partner's kids?** - Likewise, the kids could be on the receiving end of your partner's estate and may then be able to impose their will on your partnership.

Suffice it to say, it's too late to try and get an entity formed after you've died or become disabled. So do it now!

In addition to your SPE, which should be an INC or LLC, you may a need for another entity (or two) at some point in the future.

Reason #12 will make you lots of money...

Ch I. 12.

Reason #12 - Co-Author Partnerships

Even for just one boxed set!

Chris R had an idea to create a new series, outside of her normal genre, and she found the perfect writing partner to do so: Michael O, who wasn't a US citizen, was between writing projects and was in the middle of a long wait for his publisher to release his next book. Their co-writing partnership was a wonderful success, creating a new fictional world that hadn't existed before and even better, additional income for both partners. However, something was missing.

Chris volunteered to take on the back-end management of the project, and all royalties of the project went through her publishing account. Then she calculated the profit for the prior month and sent Michael his portion. Everything on the surface was perfect. However...

What if one of the following happened:
• Chris were to take a job overseas.

- Chris were to die or become disabled long term.
- Chris decided not to be so honest.

In other words, if anything happened to Chris, how would Michael enforce his end of the partnership? He has no authority: Everything is in Chris's name and there's nothing legally tying him to this project. Even if they have a partnership agreement, Michael has no authority.

Luckily for Michael, Chris is an honorable person and quite healthy, and she has an awesome husband who would take care of her business (and does currently) if something happened to her. But we cannot assume everything will work out, especially when it involves money. And the situation is often brought to a head when the partnership is more successful than what the partners thought.

The simple answer, of course, would be for them to set up a separate author entity, especially an LLC (I'll get into this in more detail in the next section).

Here's how this looks

In Chris and Michael's situation, the new entity would be:
- the owner of the series; and
- the publisher of record; and
- the owner of the copyright; and
- the owner of any trademarks related to the series or its characters; and
- the holder of the bank account that receives all royalties.
- Finally, the entity would have a separate partnership agreement that spells out what would happen if something bad occurred to either Chris or Michael.

Everyone is protected. Everything is simple.

Regardless of whether you already have (or plan to set up)

an author entity for your own publishing company (for your own works), if you plan any kind of partnership with another partner for a separate writing/publishing project, you'll want to set up another separate entity.

Consider these examples:
- Co-writing a book or a series with another author - Would your situation be like Chris and Michael's?
- Box-set partnership with other authors - How would you manage all of these partners?
- An anthology - And what if you wanted to pay based on some odd split like a percentage of the total words contributed?
- Ghost writer - Normally, you'd pay your ghost writer a flat rate. But what if you wanted to compensate your ghost writer with a percentage of royalties?
- Audiobook narrator - What if you negotiated a different royalty split than 50/50?

In all these cases, regardless of the number of partners, you could easily set up an entity that would own all elements of the project, including receipt of all royalties. You'd be the manager of the entity, and the entity would split the proceeds per whatever agreements you've set up with your partner(s).

Now onto lucky Reason #13...

Ch I. 13.

Reason #13 - Segment Projects

Especially when your book tackles a difficult subject

Brittney was a successful fantasy writer, but now she wanted to write a fictional book about a current political figure. She was motivated by a passion for that person, as well as the possibility of cashing in on a hot area of publishing. But with politics being so polarizing lately, she was fearful that publishing such a book might cause harm to her existing brands.

Have *you* wanted to write about some subject or public person or company, but been fearful of the blowback to your other writing? A new LLC could be used to segment, or split off, that book/series/article from your other author assets, protecting your other brands from any fallout such a project might entail.

There are many situations where you (or your author

assets) might be exposed to additional peril if you decide to write something outside of your normal genre or subject matter. Here are a few:

- Writing about a political figure
- Featuring a public company in a book
- Modeling one of your antagonists after a live person
- Detailing something negative about one or more religious organizations
- Launching a new series in a provocative genre (i.e., erotica)
- Experimenting with a box set with other authors who may not share your work ethic or beliefs

Regardless of the subject of your book or your reasons for covering it/them in your book, the big question you should ask yourself here is what could happen?

Any of the following possibilities:

- Could you get sued by the public figure or someone related to the organization you wrote about?
- Might rabid fans of that organization target your other books with bad reviews?
- Will people on the opposite side of the political spectrum tear you down in social media?
- Could you anger your existing fan base?

If any of these possibilities might come true, you probably want to do what Brittney did: she formed a new LLC to own and operate her new book project and her new pen name. This separates the new assets, and any problems which may accompany them, from her existing and already valuable brand assets. Then this new LLC would be listed as the copyright holder of the books and the publisher. It would be the public face of this project, instead of Brittney, even though Brittney would own and control the LLC.

Why don't you do the same?

This brings us to Reason #14...

Ch I. 14.

Reason #14 - Privacy

Keeping your name out of public scrutiny

If you want to branch out into a different genre, you may be considering a new pen name, so as to not confuse or upset the readers in your current genre. But what if you wanted to explore something more sensitive, or racy, or...? How could you do this and also hold onto your privacy?

You could still use the new pen name, but when you file a copyright, your name will be forever attached to that work, easily findable by anyone who is looking. And if you filed the copyright under your author entity's name, that would be connected to you as well.

The answer: Create a new publishing entity, set up specifically for that project and your new genre. Now you have complete privacy.

Brittney M's example comes to mind (in the previous chapter). She set up a Wyoming LLC, because the state does not require disclosure of the ownership/management information. Then she will use it to be the public face of her publishing in her new genre. She will own 1% of the new entity and her regular publishing S Corp. will own the other 99%. It's all laid out in an operating agreement, which is all private. And yet everything else is run on the back end through her main publishing company (i.e., banking, royalties, etc.).

So her new books will be written by a new author (her new pen name) published by a new company (her Wyoming LLC), and none of this is disclosed publicly. The new LLC will also own the copyrights and trademarks, but all royalties run directly through her regular author entity. Of course, the public doesn't see any of this.

There's no reason why you couldn't do exactly what Brittney did.

Other Personal Assets Too

I'm taking a quick sideline to cover another idea regarding forming an entity and your privacy. As we know, our private information has become very public. Even if we don't choose to make portions of our life public, others (especially social media enterprises and vendors we do business with) chose to "share" our information because it's profitable. As self-published authors, it's far worse, as we're always trying to get our name out there. Is there anything we can do?

That, of course, is a huge subject in itself, but one thing we can do involves forming an entity.

Your home information is part of the public record, and it's one more way that your personal information becomes connected and "out there." However, many of the wealthy own their property, including their homes, in an LLC. Why couldn't you do the same?

This would be an LLC, which is separate from your author entity, whereby it has a generic name (i.e., ABC Home Investments, LLC) and then the title is quit-claimed to the LLC. This would not eliminate your name from the public record, but it would shield it just a little more, providing you just a little more privacy in this not-very-private world.

Why... Wrap Up

There are many reasons—including a few others I didn't cover—why forming an author entity is an important step in your author business success. And if you intend to create a Self-Publishing Empire™, as I'm advocating, it is the next crucial step.

So which type of author entity is best for you?

To be able to *really* understand your choices, you need to really know what an entity is, and why an author entity will give you all the benefits we have just covered.

Ch II. What <u>REALLY</u> is an Author Entity?

And why do you need one?

Let me take you back to that moment when you first opened your self-publishing business...

Yippee!

It truly is exciting when you start a new business, no matter how big or small your ambitions might be.

However, the moment you began to write that first book (which you had planned to self-publish), or set up your author website, or created a business page on Facebook...

You became a target!

Like all business start-ups, once you have begun running your business (long before you have made any money), others will want a piece of you and your business. And if you do anything wrong, because of some unfortunate mistake, those whom you have wronged (at least in their minds) just might **go after everything you own**, and not just your fledgling business.

Now, if you are a successful indie writer, with a larger market reach, imagine how many more people might look at you as a target.

But how you own and operate your author business makes all the difference in your target.

Time to examine each option.

What <u>REALLY</u> is an author entity?

QUICK READ

Read this ONLY if you don't have time to read the chapters in this section!

In this section, I dive into what <u>really</u> is an author entity, how they work so well for authors, and what your entity choices are. Although I recommend you read each of the chapters in this section, regardless of your knowledge level, I've provided you with a Quick Read overview of the major points.

They are as follows:

> **What is a Sole Proprietorship?** - You become a sole proprietorship the moment you tell people you're in business, or you publish your first book, or you start receiving royalties in your name, and certainly when you personally own the copyright to your books. In other words you, an individual, own your business, and your business is just one of the many assets you own, like your house, car, and bank accounts. This means if you do anything (inside or outside your business), all of your assets (business AND personal) are a target.

> **What is a corporation?** - A corporation (i.e., YOU Publishing, Inc.) is like a container that you create to own and manage your writing business. This container then becomes the target for any business-related "arrows."

> **What is an LLC?** – An LLC (i.e., YOU Publishing, LLC) is similar to a corporation in that it too is a container which owns and operates your writing business assets. However, this container is more like a semi, which has some flexibility to maneuver around some of the tax targets that would have been painted on your sole proprietorship.

> **What is Corporate Personhood?** - This is the crucial root reason why you would go to the trouble of setting up an author entity: Your entity becomes a legal person, recognized as able to do much of what you can do (i.e., own businesses, take on debt, sign contracts, be sued, and even die) and by doing so, it separates itself (and all of its business assets) from you.

> **Which Entity Type is Best For YOU?** - To help you decide which entity type is best for you, I run through five different sets of criteria in comparing each entity type: Ease of set-up, Ease of management, Tax benefits, Liability protection & Pass-through benefit. In a nutshell, here is how each compares:

Sole Prop = Very easy to set up; easy to manage; yielding

some, but fewer, of the tax benefits available to other entities; no liability protection; and the new "pass-through benefit" given by the 2018 Tax Cuts & Jobs Act.

S-Corporation = Somewhat easy to set up but a complicated management structure, and with it, additional tax benefits and additional liability protection not available to sole props, but a potential to lose this protection by not following the complicated management procedures required of all for-profit corporations; and finally the same pass-through benefit.

LLC = Easy to set up; easy management structure, unlike the corporation; many of the tax benefits of the S-Corp., except all income is subject to self-employment taxes; the additional liability protection of a corporation; and the same pass-through tax benefit as the others.

Hybrid - A fourth option is given. This is an LLC, which also elects (when it makes sense) to be taxed like an S-Corporation. By doing this, it will have the same somewhat easy set-up of an S-Corp.; the ease of management of an LLC; the flexibility to enjoy the tax benefits of an S-Corp. or LLC; the liability protection of an LLC; and of course, the pass-through benefit.

In other words, I am recommending for most authors, a Hybrid LLC is best. At the same time, I strongly recommend reviewing your choices with your CPA or tax adviser, as he/she will be better able to review your own tax situation and determine the entity that works best.

If you'd like to review any of the details of each chapter, please jump to that chapter. Otherwise, now go to *Section III: Getting Ready to Form YOU Publishing, LLC.*

Ch II. 1.

What is a Sole Proprietorship?

And why it makes YOU the target

So what makes you a sole proprietorship and when do you become one?

Any one of these:

- You tell people you're going to self-publish a book; or
- You self-publish a book in your name (i.e., In the "Full Name" field, under Author/Publisher Information for your Amazon KDP account, you have listed your personal name); or
- You start receiving royalties in a bank account owned personally (even if it's a business checking account and has a DBA name on it); or
- You personally hold the copyright to your book...

You are what is called a Sole Proprietorship.

In other words, you're a single-owner business, and the ownership and income of that business is not distinguishable from you as a person. You and your business are one and the same. There's no special license you had to file with anyone to be officially recognized as a sole proprietorship: You are one the very moment you declare yourself in business.

Congratulations!

Now prepare for the onslaught, especially if you are successful.

⚖ **Wait, what if you have a DBA?**
When you set up a DBA or Doing Business As (AKA, Assumed Name or a Fictitious Name), you as a legal person (I'll get into this shortly) filed something with your county or state which says that you are operating under a name which is different than your own. It's sort of like a pen name, but for your business.... For example, "Your Name, doing business as YOU Publishing."

You are still a sole proprietor; you have only planted a flag in the ground somewhere (i.e., in your county), where you have announced that you are operating a business under this other name.

So why does any of this matter?

Because when you start a sole proprietorship, all of your assets, both personal and business, are owned and operated by the same legal person: YOU!

Do something wrong on the author side, and all of your personal assets are in jeopardy, including your home. Have someone injured at your home, and your business assets are in peril.

So when you start "Your Full Name, doing business as YOU Publishing," ownership matters.

Ch II. 2.

What is a Corporation?

And why you are protected

What if instead, you formed a corporation (i.e., YOU Publishing, Inc.) to own and operate your author business; how would that look?

Analogy: Steel Cargo Container

A corporation is like a large cargo container, in which you can place all of your author business assets. This separates your business assets from YOU personally. Once you do this, the business assets are no longer yours: they belong to the corporation (the steel cargo container), and you own the container. That way, the cargo carrier, instead of YOU, can be the focus of any arrows of liability aimed at your Self-Publishing Empire™.

Here's a more boring legal definition
(Warning: You might lapse into a coma upon reading this)

A corporation (often referred to as a Corp., or Incorporated, or Inc.) is created by filing articles of incorporation with a state, usually where the corporation primarily operates, or where the operators/owners of that corporation reside. Upon filing, a corporation has corporate personhood (see Ch II 4. For more details on what this means).

A for-profit corporation has a hierarchy of authority starting with its owners (AKA, shareholders or stockholders), who preside over the largest decisions (i.e., sale of the corp.); they elect the board of directors, who run the overall corporation's business plan and elect the officers (i.e., President, Secretary, and/or Treasurer), who take care of the day-to-day activities. Although it may sound strange, even with this hierarchy, one person can occupy all of these positions: shareholder, director, president, secretary and treasurer. Every corporation (even a single-person corporation), must follow strict corporate formalities, including holding annual meetings, which must be documented in meeting minutes (or unanimous consent decrees).

This hierarchy can be complicated and can cause further issues later on. However, if operated properly, a corporation can provide a solid way of protecting your author business.

What about an LLC?

Ch II. 3.

What is an LLC?

And what makes it flexible?

Another popular option for your author entity is a limited liability company or LLC (i.e., YOU Publishing, LLC), which would likewise own and operate your author business assets. Here is how that would look.

Analogy: Cargo Truck

An LLC is like a cargo truck which, just like a corporation, it can also hold, operate and protect all your author business assets. It too is considered a legal person. But what makes it different from a corporation is its flexibility to change its tax and management structure, helping it to avoid some specific arrows of liability altogether.

So with an LLC, if your Self-Publishing Empire™ is fired upon by someone wanting to cause harm or who wants to take from your

LLC, you have the protection of the cargo truck's shield, and it can change its stripes, moving from one tax situation or management set-up to another.

A More Legal Definition:
(It's mostly coma-free)

A limited liability company is formed by filing articles of organization with a state. And like a corporation, it has personhood. Unlike a corporation, it is more simply operated by one or more members (AKA, the owners). Unlike a corporation being forced to operate through a strict corporate hierarchy and meeting formalities (mandated by state statutes), the member(s) of an LLC operate as they see fit, controlling their operations by something called an operating agreement (think partnership agreement). This agreement is private; it can be as simple or as complex as the member(s) decide, and it can be changed by the member(s) at any time. Best of all, LLCs do not have to have formal meetings or unanimous consent decrees.

Finally, and perhaps most important, an LLC has the flexibility to be taxed as a sole proprietorship (IRS calls this "Disregarded Entity"), a partnership, or as an S Corporation. We'll talk more about this tax-flexibility in later sections.

Regardless of entity type, the key ingredient in the protection it offers is its legal personhood. Here's what I mean...

Ch II. 4.

What is Corporate Personhood?

And why is it so darned important?

When you form an author entity, it is considered by state (every state, in fact) and federal law to be its own legal person.

That means your entity could:

- **Be a business owner** - Your author entity can be the owner of one or more publishing businesses, and any other businesses as well.
- **Open up accounts** - It can open up an account with Amazon, Barnes & Noble, Ingram, etc. and publish books through their platforms.
- **Own assets** - It could possess corporate checking accounts,

copyrights to works, trademarks of brands, and publishing rights throughout the world, as well as other assets like real estate, stock, automobiles and so on.

- **Sign contracts** - That is, it can enter into contracts with people and/or other entities.
- **Be sued** - Just like any person, if an entity commits a libelous act (i.e., does something that harms someone else), the entity might be forced to pay damages and/or its assets could be in jeopardy.
- **Pay Taxes** - Or at least be required to file tax returns.
- **Die** - Just like a person, a business entity can die. In other words, its owners can kill it or the state can involuntarily kill it (i.e., for non-payment of taxes or ongoing fees).
- **Change its name** - Although entirely possible, as I will discuss in a later chapter, it's not recommended you do this.

And there is something else it can do, which you and I could not:

- **Be... immortal** - If operated correctly, your author entity can live indefinitely, outliving even you. This is how you could pass the ownership of all your author assets to family members or partners upon your death (see *Book #6: Author Legacy*).

> ⚖ **Personhood Ruling**
> As recent as 2010, the US Supreme Court (Citizens United v. Federal Election Commission) ruled that corporation & union spending may not be restricted by the government under the First Amendment, because a corporation, which is composed of individuals, deserves protection under the First Amendment, guaranteeing free speech.

Why This Matters

By setting up an author entity, and then having the entity start a new publishing business (or take possession of your already-started publishing business) and then running the business and receiving all income, your business entity is separated from you... In other words, you and your author entity are recognized as two unique and different "people," even though you may be the sole owner of this entity. Because of this, your author entity enjoys certain benefits that you wouldn't receive as a sole proprietor.

We discussed many of these reasons in the previous section.

So which of the two entity types is best for YOU, assuming you want to grow a Self-Publishing Empire™?

Ch II. 5.

Which Entity Type is Best For YOU?

Is there a "perfect" option for authors?

Okay, it's time to decide: Which type of entity should you choose for your author entity: a corporation, an LLC, or something else?

It's the question most often asked of us at SmallBiZ.com, Inc. (the filing service company I founded 20 years ago). For many reasons, this was also one of the hardest questions to answer. Knowing there were just too many variables to consider in a phone call, my staff were instructed to always kick this question back to the customer: we'd recommend they speak to their tax adviser, as usually the biggest determining factor was the tax benefits of one entity type over the other.

Don't worry, I won't kick this question back to you. Not exactly.

I'm going to give you your options, and enough information so that you can decide this on your own. I'm still going to recommend you find a good tax adviser anyway (see *The Power of an Accountant/CPA* in *What Authors Need To Know About Taxes (Self-Publishing Empire™ Book #7)*.

So how can you determine what's best for you?

How to Determine The Best Structure

We covered the basic differences of each business structure earlier in this section (*Section II. What REALLY is a business entity?*). This time, we're going to drill down and compare each structure in five specific areas:

A. **Ease of Set Up** - Is the structure or entity type easy to set up or more difficult?

B. **Ease of Management** - Once set up, is it easy to manage or more complicated? In other words, are there a lot of tasks you must do, or not very many?

C. **Tax Benefits** - Are there more tax benefits afforded one entity type vs. another?

D. **Liability Protection** - Does this type of structure protect you and your family against potential liability, and is it better or worse than the others?

E. Pass-Through Benefit - Finally, how does each structure compare when it comes to the new Pass-Through Tax Benefit offered by the newest tax law changes?

Notice that "Cost" (i.e., Cost of Set-up or Cost to Maintain) is not covered in this part of the discussion. That's because costs are specific to the state in which you form. We will cover this in great detail in the next section (*Ch III. 2. Choosing a Formation State*).

Entity/Structure Comparison

There are essentially four different structure options available to your Self-Publishing Empire™. Let's compare each now:

1. Sole Proprietorship - You become a "sole proprietorship" the moment you start trying to sell your books. Let's apply our five criteria to see how this structure works.

A. Ease of Set-up: Very easy. It's automatic when you start operating.
B. Ease of Management: Easy. There's little management required; you could even run your business out of your personal checking account.
C. Tax Benefits: Some. We'll get into more on this later. However, this structure offers the least number of tax benefits available to you, compared to those afforded other entities.
D. Liability Protection: Little to none! Your business and personal assets are all owned by you and there is no separation between you (the individual) and your business operations. In other words, if your business operation does something wrong, all of your personal and business assets are in jeopardy.
E. Pass-Through Benefit: Even sole proprietorships receive this new IRS benefit. However, all of your

business income is subject to self-employment tax. So the question is should you remain this way or set up a business entity?

2. **S-Corporation** - Also known as a Sub-Chapter S Corporation; is a pass-through entity (your net income and expenses show up on your personal tax return) and is certainly a good structure for your author entity. Let's see how it compares to a sole prop.

A. Ease of Set-up: Somewhat easy! First you form a regular for-profit corporation in a state of your choosing, and then you obtain an EIN (a social security number for your corporation), and then you elect to be taxed as an S Corporation (file Form 2553 with the IRS).

B. Ease of Management: Complicated. With an S-Corporation, you must formalize the oversight of all your major business affairs (AKA Corporate Governance). This includes: formally issuing yourself stock, formally adopting corporate bylaws (rules for governing your corporation), formally electing your director(s), who then formally elect the officers (i.e., President, Secretary and Treasurer), and you must do this at least once per year in two separate "meetings" (even if it's just you occupying all these roles) and then documenting each meeting, along with any other major decisions, in meeting minutes.

C. Tax Benefits: Absolutely! By doing all of this, you gain additional tax savings, not the least of which is avoiding self-employment taxes, by paying yourself a "reasonable" salary.

D. Liability Protection: Absolutely! But only as long as you take care of your corporate governance, thus making your business affairs separate from your personal affairs. This provides you an added layer of protection against liabilities. However, if you don't take care of your corporate governance, your corporation could be considered as no different than you (i.e., no separation), and you could lose this protection.

E. Pass-Through Benefit: Absolutely! However, if your income is below a threshold, you might not gain as much of a benefit as you would with even a sole proprietorship.

3. **Limited Liability Company or LLC** - Instead of a corporation, you could form a limited liability company to own and operate your author business assets.

   A. Ease of Set-up: Easy. Setting up an LLC is as easy as or easier than setting up an S-Corporation.

   B. Ease of Management: Easy. One simple operating agreement will care of all of your primary management issues. I'm saying it's "very easy" to manage compared to a sole prop, because of the separation; it's easier to account for what is the company's and what is yours than to have everything commingled.

   C. Tax Benefits: Yes. However, all your income may be subject to self-employment taxes.

   D. Liability Protection: Absolutely! And because your management is so much easier, there is less chance of your dropping the ball (since there's little to no corporate governance) and losing this protection.

   E. Pass-Through Benefit: Absolutely! However, if your income rises above a threshold, you may lose this benefit.

4. **Hybrid LLC** - Wouldn't it be nice if you could get the best tax benefits of an S-Corporation, but keep the management simplicity of an LLC? Now you can. This may be the best option for a Self-Publishing Empire™.

   A. Ease of Set-up: Somewhat easy. Very similar to an S-Corporation.

B. Ease of Management: Easy. One simple operating agreement will care of all of your primary management issues. Then you manage how the entity will be taxed with your tax adviser.

C. Tax Benefits: Best! Decide whether the benefits of an S-Corporation or an LLC fit your situation. And choose that.

D. Liability Protection: Absolutely! And again, just like an LLC, because your management is so easy, there is less chance of your dropping the ball and losing this protection.

E. Pass-Through Benefit: Absolutely! You'll have the benefit of an LLC's lower income threshold, but the ability to be taxed like an S-Corporation when it suits you (i.e., if your income is projected above the threshold).

Comparing Your Options

Let's do a quick review of all four options:

Entity Comparison Grid

	Sole-Prop	S-Corp.	LLC	Other
Ease of Set-up	X	X	X	X
Ease of Management	X		X	X
Improved Tax Benefits		X	X	X
Liability Protection		X	X	X
Maximized Pass-Through Tax Benefits				X

So what is this "Other" Hybrid" option?

It is an LLC. But when it's the appropriate time, the LLC elects with the IRS to be taxed like an S Corporation (for federal tax purposes only).

Narrowing Down Your Entity Type

As you can see, I am purposely pointing you in the direction of what I am calling a Hybrid LLC. And the reason for this is because the new tax law has made this decision even easier.

> The new tax law has changed everything when it comes to making this decision. Because a Self-Publishing Empire™ is considered a favorable business type and therefore its income is considered Qualified Business Income, the best entity becomes the Hybrid LLC.

Depending on your income, you'll have the flexibility of remaining an LLC, taxed like a sole proprietorship, but with all the other tax benefits an entity enjoys. But you'll also be able to change to an S-Corporation for federal taxation (by sending in two forms to the IRS), if and when it makes sense to do so. I'm staying away from the details on this one. Trust me when I say the new tax law is so complicated that most tax professionals have not figured all the details of this yet, at least as of the time I write this.

The beauty of this best-of-all-worlds option is that you have some flexibility that you wouldn't have with a corporation.

Note: There are other entity options, but for 99% of the authors and self-publishers, these are not applicable. However, it is even more reason why after you think you have decided, you should go see your tax adviser and review your choices once more.

The Tax Benefits of Each

I have purposely brushed over the tax benefit specifics of each entity type. This is for two reasons: 1) I plan to cover more detail in *What Authors Need To Know About Taxes (Self-Publishing Empire™ Book #7)*; and 2) the complexities of taxes are best left for the eggheads who live and breathe taxes. Going back to my chapter on trying to DIY everything, this is one area in which you absolutely should seek help from an expert. The final ruling on the most recent update to the tax code was over 170 pages. I read the whole thing twice and was sure my brain might explode. This stuff is ridiculously complex. Only with an expert, who can learn the specifics of your situation, can you hope for a careful assessment and a plan for what you should do next. My goal is to help you to understand the basics and ask smart questions of your tax adviser.

NOTE: There are always exceptions to what I am recommending. For instance, if you have partners (with different tax issues or who are not citizens of the US), you want to utilize profit sharing plans, your state's tax schedules might be substantially higher for an LLC (i.e., California), and lots of other variables, which can make each individual author situation so different. The bottom line here—in case I haven't stressed it enough—is to find a good tax adviser in your state. That tax adviser will look at your specific needs and apply those and the tax benefits available to your best entity choice.

Okay, do you have an entity type in mind? If you do, let's get ready to form YOU Publishing LLC (or INC).

Ch III. Prepare to Form YOU Publishing, LLC

Get ready to form your author entity

Authors are notorious for jumping into a writing project without looking forward to what lies ahead. Most just write, at best only knowing where they'll end up but not knowing how they'll get there. As a writer, you would be called a "panster." And this is an acceptable practice, for writing.

But as author business owners, pantsting will only lead you to problems.

By now, you have your entity type selected and you are now ready to form YOU Publishing, LLC (Or YOU Publishing, INC). But there are a few more actions/decisions you must take before you can actually form your author entity.

They are:

1. **Choosing an Entity Name and Why It's So Important -** Even if you have one, please read this chapter!

2. **Choosing a Formation State!** - You only have 51 to choose from. Again, read this chapter to make sure you have considered all possibilities.

3. **DIY or hire the pros** - A few thoughts on whether your time is better spent writing and hiring pros or learning how to DIY.

4. **Your Entity Outline** - Outline the who, what and where of your outline

5. **Final Preparation** - A worksheet

6. **Step-By-Step Instructions** - On how to create YOU Publishing LLC.

Next, let's review what makes a good entity name, why it is so important to choose right, whether it's even available, and then make sure it's not stupid.

Prepare to Form YOU Publishing, LLC
QUICK READ

Read this ONLY if you don't have time to read each of the chapters in this section!

At this point, you've determined the type of entity you want to form, but there are a few more actions/decisions you must take before you can actually form your author entity.

Below is an overview of the key points in each chapter in this section.

1. **Why is Your Entity Name So Important?** - I warn that this may be your most important decision, so again, I stress reading this chapter. The biggest reason why you want to choose right the first time is because it is too costly to do over again later. So choose right the first time. Here are the elements of a good name: It is memorable, it

describes what your business does, it does NOT include your personal name, it's not confusing, it is unique, it is scalable, it must have brandability, and therefore be eligible to be trademarked, it cannot already be used (in your state, at USPTO.gov, and in general, findable on Google). Finally, I recommend not to choose a stupid name and I offer several examples... If you don't want to see what these are, that's your fault.

2. **Choosing a Formation State** - You must choose a state in which you will form your author entity. And as I point out, with DC (considered a state), you have fifty-one states to choose from. After describing a few definitions, I point out some of the factors you should consider when choosing your formation state. These include costs to set up, costs to maintain in that state, privacy and finally your residency. For the vast majority of authors, you will want to choose the state you primarily reside in.

There are of course further questions which may make this decision more difficult: having a partner who is a resident in a different state, not being a US citizen, being a resident of more than one state, and the prospect of moving to another state in the future.

To make it easy for those having questions, I offer a logic grid of yes/no questions, which should lead you to the right choice.

3. **Get Help or DIY?** - Once you've reached this point, I illustrate why using a professional filing service might be better than doing it yourself. I offer a way to calculate the value of your time, so that you can then apply this number to the cost of hiring someone to do your author entity filing to see if it is in fact worth using your valuable time to DIY your own filing.

In my example, I came up with the value of each hour of my time being worth nearly $50 to $100 per hour, based solely on what I would make to write my next book, instead of using my time on activities such as this. Even if we halved these numbers, I argue it would still be a better proposition to hire someone vs. DIY.

4. **Filing Worksheet - LLC** - Next, assuming you have chosen to form an LLC, I provide you a worksheet you can use to prepare all the information you will need to do your filing, regardless of whether you DIY or hire a professional to do your filing. If you chose an INC, move to the next chapter summary.

   Rather than summarizing the worksheet here, I recommend you take a look at this chapter to see the overview of the worksheet or go to SelfPublishingWorkshop.com and get your copy of this worksheet.

5. **Entity FAQs** - There are just a few more questions I want to clear up, whether you were wondering these or not. Here are the questions and the simple answers:

   Q: What creates an entity? A: Filing a simple document with the appropriate state agency.
   Q: When does an entity exist? A: The date the filing is accepted.
   Q: Do you need an attorney? A: No! But there are times when you might want one.
   Q: Do you have to be a US Citizen? A: No! But you might have some difficulty setting up a bank account.
   Q: What documents do you need? A: Besides the appropriate worksheet, just your checkbook or CC.

6. **Step-By-Step INC/LLC Filing** - Then I give you a step-by-step overview of the process to form your new entity, including a screen shot of an actual entity filing I did online in Florida, just to show how easy it is.

   Then I give you the steps to actually file yours on your own, starting with going to the Appendix, finding your state, and then following the instructions.

If you'd like to review any of the details of each chapter, please jump to that chapter. Otherwise, go now to *Section IV: Immediately After: What You Must Do!*

Ch III. 1.

Why is Your Entity Name So Important?

This may be your most important decision,
so take your time to decide

Heading to the Midwest to visit family, I ran across an in-law on my flight. I said, "Lucy, is that you?" She said, "I go by Lucette now." I had to hold back my laughter: This was a woman who had already formally changed her name once and informally several other times. Who could keep up?

Don't be a Lucette!

Being a part of a company that has formed over 100,000 business entities, I always found it odd how lightly business owners approach naming their own entities. It was like they had Lucette's attitude, thinking they could change their name to anything they want, whenever they want.

Technically this is true. In reality, it is not! It would be much worse for your Self-Publishing Empire™.

Understand this: Naming your author entity right now is one of the most important actions you'll take! You absolutely need to get this right. The first time!

Your entity's name is what your business will be identified by; it will be what represents you; it will be the cornerstone of YOUR own business reputation; and although you can change the name at any time, the repercussions of making changes later on are too huge to consider. In other words, this is damned important right now!

Too costly to do over

Let us assume you form your author entity, then a year later you want to change its name to something "even better." At that point, you will have destroyed over one year of branding your SPE's name to your books, to your online presence, to your social media platforms, and to everything else you do. And the logistical costs of such a change would be monumental. They include: state fees to make the change to your entity, changing its record with the IRS and any other taxing agencies, changing it with your bank, vendors and creditors; changing it on your website, and/or maybe having to get a new domain name, email, etc.; changing it on every book you've published on print, eBook and audiobook, and not only with each publishing platform, but within each book; changing it with Bowker for your ISBNs; and those are just a few of the changes you would have to make. Others you can't change include your copyrights and trademarks, which will be permanently set to your original entity name.

Are you starting to understand how crucial this is?

Good!

Now, let's take some time to figure out what you author entity name should be.

NOTE: If you've already got your name figured out, I'd still strongly suggest you consider each element of what I have outlined for you below.

How to choose the best entity name, now!

Would you recommend T&A Pool Service, Inc. to your neighbors? The owners of this company had no idea why this name might have a negative connotation to it. They were just using their founders' initials, "Todd" and "Andrew." After the rather obvious sexual reference the name might have conferred to some potential customers was pointed out, they opted to switch the abbreviation around to "A & T Pool Service, Inc."

There are several elements your business name should possess. If it possesses them all, you probably have a great business name. Here they are, in order:

- **Memorable** - Can people remember the name, or will customers/vendors always be asking, what was that name again?
  Avoid: overly generic names and letter abbreviations

- **Describes what your business does** - Including in your author entity name a word such as "publishing" or "press" or even "books" ensures that anyone hearing the name understands what the entity does. This again goes to your SPE's image.

Avoid: something too specific (i.e., "digital books" would be limiting to other formats)

- **Don't just use your personal name** - It may be tempting to use your own name in your author entity name, and in fact you may be thinking (because of my use of "YOU Publishing, LLC") that I am advocating this. But if you use your name (or a pen name) in the publishing name, you have less latitude to maneuver later (i.e., take on other authors, expand into other genres, etc.). And you potentially defeat the whole "Sole-Propism" issue we discussed in Chapter I. 6. Remember, you are creating a Self-Publishing Empire™.

- **Not confusing** - Your business name should be obvious and lack anything which might confuse people or make it more difficult to remember.
Avoid: double meanings, strange spellings of words, or odd punctuation.

- **Unique** - It's much better to be the only one on the block or better yet, in the universe, with a specific business name. And sometimes all it takes to make your business name unique is the addition of one word. You may have no choice based on what's available in your state of formation. However, for reasons mentioned above, you don't want to get too unique, as it might be difficult to remember or pronounce, or be plain confusing.
Avoid: foreign words (i.e., other languages), unless there's a strong reason for it.

- **Scalable** - Likewise, you don't want your business name limiting what your SPE can grow into. You want a business name that can scale up to something bigger

than perhaps you can even imagine right now.
Avoid: specific state or city references.

- **Brandable** - If you've accomplished the first five elements of your business name, it will be brandable. That's a great thing! Congrats, you're almost done.

- **Trademarkable** - If it's brandable, you can file a federal trademark on it to protect it. We will dive into more detail on this subject, in *Book #3: Protecting Your Intellectual Property*.

- **Not already used** - Here's a tough one. Part of being unique is having a business name that isn't currently being used by another business. You should avoid this at all costs. However, this can more difficult than it sounds because business entities are formed on a state level. This certainly means searching your state's entity name database, but it is not exactly feasible to search all fifty-one states (DC is considered a state because you can file an entity there). Here is where you should check to make sure your corporate name is not already currently being used:

  - **State Database** - Check the availability of your business name in whichever state you are forming your business entity. In the Appendix, you'll find the link to do this name check for every state. If your proposed business name is an exact match with an existing and active entity, you'll need to choose another one. Often this can be as simple as changing one word in the name. Again, don't worry too much if the business entity's name is already in use in another state... yet.
  HINT: When you search, do not use a corporate name ending. For example, if your proposed name

is "In Your Face Publishing, LLC" search "In Your Face Publishing."

- **Trademark Office** - It is really important that you make sure that someone hasn't already registered your prospective business name with the US Patent and Trademark Office. If your name is registered, you should choose another one, or modify the name such as that it still fulfills all the elements above. Go here to check names with USPTO: https://www.uspto.gov/trademarks-application-process/search-trademark-database.
  HINT: When you search, try going to the root of the name. In other words, if "In Your Face Publishing, LLC" is your proposed name, search the USPTO for "In Your Face" and see what comes up associated with the area of publishing. If there's an active trademark for "In Your Face" in the area of publishing, you might not be able to use the name at all.

- **Google** - Try Googling the proposed business name to see if it is in use. When you search be sure to put your search query in quotes. This is telling the search engine that you want exactly what's between the quotation marks. For example, if you search for "In Your Face Publishing" (don't search the full corporate name), then the search results will only contain the indexed web pages which specifically mention that name.

Did your name pass the muster? If it did, you may have found your SPE's business name. But before you move onto the next chapter, consider this:

Don't Choose a Stupid Name

As mentioned in the foreword to this book, one of my businesses has been involved in the formation of at least one hundred thousand entities. And although I haven't seen them all, I've seen my share of stupid names.

To demonstrate how some people just don't think when it comes to naming their entity, here are a few examples of some of the names of INCs and LLCs that we've created for people or have been asked to create.

- Mary's Coming, LLC - This was a Catholic organization, the founders of whom didn't understand the sexual double meaning of the name until I pointed it out to them.
- Gain Green, LLC - Is this offering some product which is going green or is it going bad (i.e., gangrene)? I recommended amputating this name.
- Double D's Sweet Treats, Inc. - It's just a bakery, but I don't think most people will think of supple bread or ballooning donuts when they see the first two words.
- FYB, LLC - Yes, the customer said it was named in honor of his ex-wife, whom he did not care for.
- Sexy Taco Dirty Cash, LLC — The owners of this restaurant thought they were being cute, but is this really the brand you want to sell for your taco restaurant?

If your name passed all of these considerations, you're done! But I want to cover just one other area that comes up often.

DBA's/Assumed Business Names - A business entity (or person) that uses a name which is different than their own is "doing business as" or operating under an "assumed business name." This is often done when that enterprise branches off into a different direction or wants to add a new brand or asset and at the same time, be identified by that brand. For instance, if I start calling myself In Your Face Publishing before I've formed my business entity by the same name, I would legally be identified as "Michael Banner doing business as In Your Face Publishing." If I were an entity and I got into designing covers for authors, I might file a DBA (with my county or state) so that my entity is connected to that name.

This is one of the reasons why I suggest that you choose a name which is scalable, so that you don't have to worry about filing a DBA in the future.

Okay, you've got a name that's memorable; it describes your publishing business correctly; it's not confusing; it's unique and yet scalable; it's brandable and trademarkable; it's not been used by anyone yet–you've checked practically everywhere; and it is definitely not stupid. Before you form your business entity, you need to decide in which state you are going to file the documents.

Let us find out which is best for you.

Ch III. 2.

Choosing a Formation State

Which one should you choose?

© SelfPublishingEmpire.com

You are ready to form your author entity and move forward with your Self-Publishing Empire™; you know your entity type; you even have your entity name researched and chosen. You have one more decision to make...

But fifty-one choices.

> A business entity is formed on the state level, and so you have fifty-one (51) states to choose from (DC is considered a "state" for this purpose).

The easiest choice is to select the state in which you reside (i.e., paying personal taxes to that state) **and where you operate your business**. That's what most business owners do. In fact, perhaps 90% or more of all small business owners (including authors) do this. And if this works for you, you could probably skip the rest of this chapter.

But what if...

- Your state's fees are too expensive?
- You don't reside in the US?
- You plan on moving to another state?
- You reside in two states (two places you call home)?
- Your co-author/business partner resides in another state or country?

Hopefully, you can see why this question is not always easy to answer. If you are not sure which state to choose, I'm going to give you an easy formula to determine which is best for you and your author entity. Even if you have already decided on your state, let me recommend you review this chapter to ensure you have not missed something.

Definitions

Domestic Entity

Whichever state your author entity calls home (i.e., the state in which it is formed), your entity is then considered "domestic" to that state. And the entity is called a Domestic Entity, and that state becomes the entity's "home state" as well. In other words, your author entity is like a resident of that "home state." Just like you, depending on that state's laws, your entity may have to pay taxes and file a tax return and/or report to that state *every year* to comply with all of that state's rules.

Foreign Entity

When an entity operates in another state (we'll call that state, "State B"), which is different than the state in which it was formed (call this "State A"), that entity is known in as a "foreign entity" to State B. This most often happens when an entity wants to open a physical office/store in State B. In that case, that entity must file for "authority" (also referred to as "foreign authority") to do business in State B. You may be thinking, "What the heck do I care? I'm never going to open a store, much less an office in another state." But you may.

Here's how.

 Could you be running a foreign operation?
Because of a recent Supreme Court decision, the rules to determine when an entity is "operating" in a foreign state falls on that state (i.e., State B). For instance, if you were to operate a bookstore on your website, selling your books and SWAG to readers all over the US (I'm not going to even cover other countries), one or more states outside of your entity's "home state" may decide that your entity must file for authority, file annual tax filings, and pay sales (and other taxes) to that state.

Don't freak out!

The good news is if you only sell a few items on your website, you probably don't have any worries. But it's worth having a conversation with your accountant/tax adviser every year, to review your activities and find out where other states are causing problems. And if you do wish to continue selling other stuff from your website, consider selling through an affiliate program instead (i.e., Amazon), or even set up an Amazon shop (they handle all of the taxation stuff). Or you may wish to subscribe to or buy software or use a platform that helps you take care of this more easily.

Even if you don't sell products on your website...

Concepts to Consider When Choosing a State

Costs to Set Up
Forming your author entity can be fairly simple, and costs fairly little in most states. In every case, you're paying a single "filing fee" to set up your business entity. This filing fee ranges from as

little as $50 to as much as $725 (or even more). When deciding on your formation state (that state in which you form your domestic business entity), the amount you'll pay for the filing fee is part of your entity set-up costs.

Other set-up costs can include the following:
> **Post-filing fees** - Additional filing and related fees that some states require you to submit relatively quickly after you've formed your entity.
> **Filing service fees** - If you use an attorney or professional filing service (like SmallBiZ Filings), they will charge you a fee to file your documents and pay your filing fee to the state.
> **Registered agent** - This is the legal contact of the entity in its formation state. If you are a resident of the state, you can act as the entity's registered agent. If not, you will probably have to pay a third party to act as agent. Fees range from $50 to $250 per year for this service.
> **Ancillary services** - If you require assistance to set-up your EIN (done through the IRS) or with document or record keeping set-up or with your operating agreement (see *Chapter V. 2. Next Steps for LLC's*), you will have some other fees associated with this.

Costs to Maintain
After your entity is set up, there will be ongoing costs to maintain your entity, which you'll want to factor into your business planning.

Here are some of those costs:
> **State taxes** - If you form an LLC, and it is owned and operated by one person, most states don't require that you pay state taxes, as you often do this on your personal side. But a lot of states do, and some charge exorbitant minimum taxes, even if your entity doesn't

earn a dime. California, for instance, charges LLCs $800 in minimum taxes each year (on April 15th) and another $800 within four months after the LLC is registered. This may lead you to form a corporation instead, which has fewer minimum taxes in its first year of operation.

> **Annual Report filing fees** - Most every state requires that your INC/LLC file an annual report of some sort, along with another fee, each year.

> **Registered agent** - Again, if you have a third-party registered agent, you'll want to consider your fees

> **Accounting fees** - Your tax situation (on the federal and state sides) will be a little more complicated once you form an entity. Unless you're an accountant and you're very comfortable handling all the IRS and state reporting, you'll want to have a professional take care of this. You'll pay fees for filing tax returns (federal and state) and sometimes payroll reporting, which may occur with an entity being taxed as an S Corp.

Privacy

I hate to tell you this, but once you form a business entity, some of your information is made public and you'll start to receive solicitations from multiple companies. Some will be legit business offers, but many will be fraudulent (watch out for those that claim your entity owes more money—it is usually not true). There are a few things you can do to avoid this.

Yes, you could form an entity in a state where there is little to no public disclosure of your ownership (i.e., Delaware and Wyoming). However, operating that entity in your own home state (i.e., doing the banking, creating your books, etc.) will often require a "foreign" registration in your state of operation (remember, your state of operation would be different than its formation state in this case), and that almost always involves disclosure of the management and/or the ownership.

However, there may be a good reason to form your author entity in one of these two states...

One Strategy - Consider this if your home state's costs are too high:

Let's say that you reside in California (or another home state where costs to form and maintain are higher than you'd like to pay before you know for sure whether this self-publishing thing is going to work out. For instance, your costs will include at least $1600 in franchise taxes in the first 14 months to form an LLC in California. And that's before your author business has made any money. Instead, consider forming your LLC in Wyoming. The state fee is only $100, and the annual costs are just $50 (annual report fee and no taxes) and as little as $99 per year registered agent fee (offered by SmallBiZ Filings). The negative is you won't be able to set up your entity's bank accounts yet (you'd have to use a personal account), but when you decide that you want to move ahead, you can formally domesticate your Wyoming LLC into a California LLC and then you can open your bank account and reimburse your LLC all of the business costs. This might be a solution if you're a year or so away from reaching this conclusion, and in the meantime you are operating your author entity (for the reasons we discussed), but for a much lower cost initially than if you formed directly in California.

Note (for California residents): you could also form a California corporation instead, which has lower upfront franchise taxes (as little as zero for the first 12 months). Then when it makes sense, you could "convert" it to a California LLC. In other words, you have options, even if you are in a high-tax state like California.

Still not sure which state to form in?

How to Choose Your Formation State - Ask yourself these questions:

1. Can you afford the costs to form an INC/LLC in the state you reside?

> If you're not sure, find the answer by either:
>
> A. Going to your state's website (find links in the Appendix to this book)
>
> B. Asking a filing services company like SmallBiZ Filings.

> **IF YES, go to #2**
>
> **IF NO**, review the chapter in the Foreword, Are You A Real Business... or Hobby?

2. Can you afford the cost to maintain an INC/LLC (in your state) for the next one to two years (or until your SPE is profitable)?

> If you're not sure, find the answer by either:
>
> A. Going to your state's website (find links in the Appendix to this book)
>
> B. Asking a filing services company, like SmallBiZ Filings.

> **IF YES**, go to #4
>
> **IF NO**, go to #3

3. Consider the cost to form and maintain an INC/LLC (outside of your state) for the next one to two years: is that affordable?

> Form a new LLC for as little as $50 in state fees and maintain it for as little as $124 per year. Then, when your entity starts making money, you can look to moving it to your state. This could minimize your upfront costs to start, especially if you're months away from receiving enough royalties to cover these expenses. The drawback to this method is it may cost you more to move the entity back to your state later. Find out your options to know if this is viable for you.

If you're not sure of the answer, find out by either:
A. checking out other state websites and researching their costs (find links in the Appendix to this book); or
B. ask a filing services company, like SmallBiZ Filings.

IF YES, go to #4
IF NO, go back to #1

4. You know you can afford the costs to form and maintain an entity in your state (or an Alternate State); now it's time to form your entity!

Before you form your author entity, you need to examine if this is a process you want to DIY, or if you want to hire this service out. Consider this...

Ch III. 3.

Get Help or DIY?

Time vs. Money

John D., a friend of mine, ran a successful insurance agency and was generally a smart businessman. After more than a year of my telling him why he should incorporate his agency, he told me that he did this, but on his own (I had offered to have SmallBiZ Filings do it for only $25 plus costs). Turns out he over-paid for publishing (which was an AZ requirement then) by doing it on his own.

Can You Become An Expert at Everything?

There are two great considerations for any and every activity, especially when it comes to your author business: Do it yourself (DIY) or hire an expert to do it for you.

There are certainly some skills you can quickly learn about and become expert at, and then that skill will be useful for years to come for your author business. Marketing is good example of one of those skills. You could hire that out, but then you are always dependent upon those "experts" to do your marketing for you. For many, it would be better to learn this so that you can become expert at marketing your own books.

But I think we can agree there are some skills that you might not be able to become expert at, even given enough time. I know, for instance, that I cannot DIY my own book covers. God knows I have tried. And even if I took the months or years to ramp up my skills to the point I could call myself "expert," I'm sure I was not blessed with the God-given talent to make it happen. Some skills are like that, while others are definitely doable, they just take a long time to become expert and have no utility for the future after you have learned them.

So what about forming your business entity?

My friend John did it himself, instead of using experts (one he knew personally), and it ended up costing him not only more money, but a lot of his professional time. And herein lies a crucial business question you should apply to anything and everything you do in your business...

What's your time worth?

Even if you *really* feel like you can execute an activity at or near the same quality level as an "expert" in that field, why would you do so based on the value of your own professional time?

Based on Your Profession

You may then ask, "Wait, I'm an author; how could I possibly know what my time is worth?

This is an excellent question, and it's one I asked myself when trying to figure out the value of writing another book versus doing a book fair. If you're interested, I posted an article about my experience on my website (http://author.mlbanner.com/picks-shovels-my-observations-at-book-fair/). It was that discernment which forced me to sit down to figure this out for myself. Here is what I found:

Value of Each Writing Hour

	Words/HR	Total Words	Total Hours	Value of Each Book $10,000 To $20,000	
Writing - 1st Draft	500	60000	120		
Writing - 2nd Draft	1000	60000	60		
Final Re-Write	3000	60000	20		
Prep & Marketing			10		
Total Hours			210		
Value of Each Hour of My Time:				$48 To	$95

Even if my math is off and it takes you twice as long to write a book and/or you are only going to make half of the income on each book that I had estimated, that still means your time is worth between $12 and $24 per hour. Now realistically try to figure out how much time it would take you to learn and then expertly do that activity vs. hiring an expert to do it quickly and professionally.

Based on Hiring

My friend John spent maybe five hours trying to figure out and then form his entity for himself. Even if his professional time is worth $0/ hour, and ignoring what he over-paid by doing it himself, he would have only spent $25 for my company's fee (he would also be spending the costs for state fees and publishing whether he did it himself or used SmallBiZ Filings)... Did you do the math yet? John valued his time at only $5 per hour ($25/ 5 hours).

You might then say, "I have to DIY everything because I can't afford to do otherwise!" Again, that's fine, but remember that means you're not busy creating a Self-Publishing Empire™ yet; you're working on a hobby that wants to become a business.

Either way, you will still need to consider how much productivity you would give away to try and become an expert at a skill you may never use again

What's next?

Whether you go the DIY or professional route, it is now time to put together all the information you will need to complete your filing.

Next up is a worksheet to help you with this.

Ch III. 4.

Filing Worksheet - LLC

Fill this out to make your filing process easy

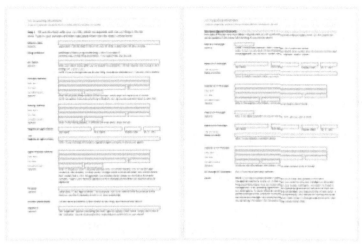

(See "Forms" in Appendix for this worksheet)

Below is an overview of an Organizing Worksheet, which I recommend you fill out before you attempt to either order from a filing service or DIY.

NOTE: You can download a copy of the actual fill-in-the-blanks worksheet for either the INC or LLC. Go to "Forms" in the Appendix for more details.

The following is based on a Florida LLC filing, but the information is virtually the same for most states' LLC filings. So where you see "Florida," just substitute your state.

Organizer Worksheet

Here is the information you will need to provide for your filing:

- **Effective Date**: When you want your entity to officially begin.
  Options: Leave blank = let the state fill this in for your OR enter a date within 90 days of today.

- **Filing Addition**s: Do you want to add anything to your formation filing?
  Options: Certificate of Status (or good standing) – Only if you need it!
  Certified Copy (of the filing documents) – You'll get a filed copy anyway.

- **LLC Name**: The name you've chosen for your LLC
  Options: Enter your name choice (after you've checked its availability). Florida requires that include a name ending (i.e., LLC or L.L.C.).
  NOTE: If you're having a service do your filing, consider an alternative if first choice is NOT available.

- **Principal Address** - Enter the physical/street address of the business, which does NOT have to be in Florida.
  NOTE: Be careful of browser pre-filling in fields for you; ignore and manually enter in each field.

- **Mailing Address**: Enter the physical/street address of the business, which does NOT have to be in Florida.
  Options: Enter in the mailing address, if different OR if the same, check the box.

- **Registered Agent:** Enter in the person (and FL physical address) who is a Florida resident and will be the legal contact for the company. In other words, if a legal notice must be delivered, who should receive this?

  Options: Usually that is YOU! Do not enter in a company name, unless you've hired a third-party company. Type in your name as signature where indicated (some states will require a physical signature).

- **Purpose (of LLC):** What is the purpose of the LLC?

  Options: Leave blank = "Any legal purpose." List a purpose only if you want to limit the purpose of the entity or you find it necessary to list it (i.e., book publishing).

- **Contact Info:** List the name and address of the contact for this filing and future annual reports.

- **Signature:** One person must "sign," acknowledging the filing and that the info is true.

  Options: The "organizer" (person submitting this form) signs by typing in their name. Usually this is one of the "members" but can be anyone who is authorized to submit this on your behalf.

Info About The LLC's Principals

(The state of Florida—and most states—requires that you set up and disclose the initial principals of the LLC. This public info can be updated in the future with the filing of your annual report)

- **1st Principal Title:** What is the authority of the 1st person listed?

  Options: AMBR = Authorized Member; MGR = Manager; AP = Authorized Person

  Note: If your LLC will always (in the

foreseeable future) have owners who will own and be a part of management, you will fill in "AMBR" here. "Authorized Member" means "owner."

- **1st Prin. Name:** Can be an individual's name or the name of another entity

- **1st Prin. Address:** Can be in any state or country

- **2nd Prin. Info:** List the title, name and address of the 2nd person

  Options: Fill this out ONLY if you have a partner. If it's just you, you're done!

- **Other Principals:** List this info ONLY if you have three to six total partners.

  NOTE: If you have multiple partners, especially six or more, they probably won't have management authority in the LLC. In that case, you would list only your managers on the public filing documents (here), and you would reflect your owners (members), who aren't involved in management, in an Operating Agreement. The Operating Agreement is private and not filed with any state agency; it would reflect all ownership percentages, and responsibilities of each party. A perfect example of this would be in a boxed set partnership. Only the person running the boxed set should be a manager and would be listed as "MGR" in the 1st Principal area of the form, and the remaining "Principals" (for the public filing) would not be listed.

What about Corporations?

I've left the corporation worksheet explanation out of this chapter, because the process of collecting information and entering it into a state form is virtually the same, and most of you will be forming an LLC and not a corporation.

If however, you are forming a corporation, I have provided a Corporation Worksheet as well (see "Forms" in Appendix for details) Just download the worksheet, fill it out and you should be ready.

Okay, a few more questions to answer and then it is time to file.

Ch III. 5.

Entity FAQs

You will be glad we covered them

Because they have not been covered, allow me to give you answers to a few of the most common questions about entity creation.

What creates an author entity?

The process of submitting Articles of Incorporation (for an INC) or Articles of Organization (for an LLC), to the appropriate state agency with your formation state is what creates your author entity. This can be done with a physical fill-in-the-blank document that your state can provide you or more commonly now (if your formation state offers it) submitting a form digitally online.

When does an entity officially exist?

Your entity usually begins or starts (AKA: Formation Date)

on the date you submit to the state, though sometimes this happens after the state processes your submittal. The approval time can be instantaneous, or it might take several weeks. For YOUR state's filing time estimate, check out the Appendix for a detailed state-by-state listing.

Regardless of what is the "official" date, once your articles are approved by your formation state, your entity exists, and you are ready to do business!

Do I need an attorney?

No... Well, mostly. Unless you're creating a new South Carolina Corporation, which requires the signature of an attorney (guessing attorneys wrote that law!), you do NOT have to have an attorney involved in any part of the filing process. That is unless YOU want one.

Attorneys have their place, especially if you are setting up a partnership: You might want help setting up your partner agreements.

Do you have to be a US citizen?

No. There is nothing which requires that you reside in or become a resident or citizen of the US to form a US corporation or limited liability company. The IRS (Internal Revenue Department) will even issue your foreign-owned US entity the equivalent of a Social Security number, which you'll need to file US taxes.

You will have a little difficulty, however, opening a US bank account. But we'll get into that in the next section, after you file.

What documents/information do you need to have on hand?

Other than some information and your checkbook (or credit card), nothing.

All right, it is time...

Ch III. 6.

Step by Step

Here's what to do

It's time to form your author entity! Yeah!

You should have already chosen or done the following:

- entity type (INC or LLC); and
- entity name (to which you've applied all the criteria discussed in *Ch III. 1.*); and
- formation state; and
- whether you are DIY or using a filing service; and
- your worksheet is filled out.

So let's get 'er done!

My instructions below are the same whether you are going to have someone do everything for you or you DIY. Are you ready?

The process of DIY forming a corporation or LLC

1. **Check Name availability** via the state link in the Appendix; and then

2. **Prepare** (fill out) a form (either paper or online) with the info from your worksheet and sign it (either physically or digitally) as instructed; and then

3. **Pay** the state's filing fee (usually by credit card or check if physically mailing docs); and finally

4. **Submit** to the state.

That's it.

I guess I could add a 5th step, which is "Wait for it to be completed."

So how do you complete #2 Prepare (fill out) a form?

Step I: Go to your state's page in the Appendix to either file online or download the paper forms and instructions.

Step II: Complete the form using your worksheet and submit to the state.

Example:
If you need a little more help to see how easy the process is, I've provided screenshots for the filing process in Florida, which is pretty similar to other state filing agencies.

1. Go to the website: dos.myflorida.com/sunbiz/ & click on the link, "New Florida LLC" (under Filing Services)

2. Click on "File or Correct Florida LLC Articles of Organization

3. Select the box that you accept their terms, and then click on "Start New Filing" button.

4.Enter in all the information you prepared on your Organizer Worksheet...

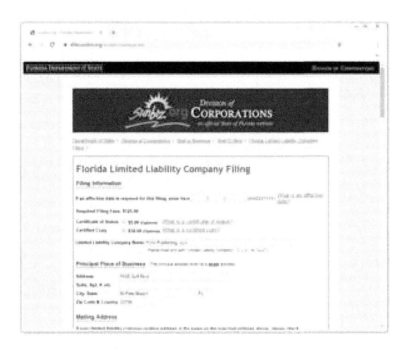

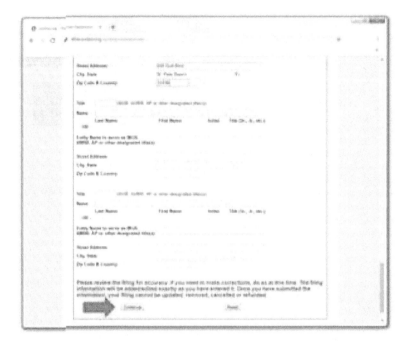

5. After you've filled out the entire form, click the "Continue" button to review your answers. If you have made any mistakes, you would use your browser back button to make your changes. If everything is acceptable, click the "Continue" button to get the form ready for submittal to the state.

6. You'll be warned that you can't change any of the information if you go forward. Click "OK" and then you'll be given a screen with an assigned Document Number. Write this down, or better yet, print this so you have it for later, if you need to follow up on it with the state (they'll ask for the Document Number). Click "Continue" to pay.

7. You will next be asked to pay: Click on the "Credit Card" button. In the credit card screen, enter in your CC info and click the "Continue" button.

8. Verify the credit card information and submit. You are done! You'll see a confirmation page (you don't need to print this). Almost instantly, you will receive an email confirmation of your filing.

Now, the only thing you can do is wait for the state to process your filing. As of my writing this, Florida filings were taking around two weeks to process. You'll receive an email of your approval then, to the email address you used in the Correspondence area of the filing form.

Once you have filed your LLC, and you've received the approval, move onto the next Section IV. *Immediately After: What You Must Do!*

Ch IV. Immediately After: What You Must Do!

This is where your Self-Publishing Empire™ really begins

YOU Publishing, LLC (Or YOU Publishing, INC.) is now a thing and you are on your way to developing your Self-Publishing Empire™.

Now what?

Many start-up businesses stop here and assume everything is good. But here is the problem...

Remember the concept of "Corporate Personhood"? You know, where YOU Publishing, LLC and YOU are considered two separate legal persons? Well that only continues if YOU also treat YOU Publishing, LLC as separate from you.

> If your author entity is NOT maintained as a separate legal person, and not a proxy for you, then all of the benefits your entity enjoys could be stripped away from it.

In other words, if you don't do a few things right away, and every year after this, your author entity might be in jeopardy. The good news is that the immediate things are all pretty easy. But you must do them now, even before you can officially start operating your entity.

What follows is a fairly brief but comprehensive list of what you need to do next to get your author entity ready to do business. Unlike previous sections, because everything covered in the next few chapters is so important, there will not be a Quick Read overview. You must do all that follows:

1. **Next Steps For Your LLC** - What must be done for a brand-new LLC!

2. **Next Steps for Your INC** (If you formed a corporation instead) - What must be done for a brand-new INC!

3. **Agreements and Contracts** - There are at least three crucial agreements you must write up, and all three are between you and your author entity!

4. **Getting a Tax ID#** - Just like we have Social Security Numbers, your entity needs its tax ID before it can take in its first penny!

Once these items are completed, you can begin operations.

Here are the next few things you must do...

Ch IV. 1.

Next Steps For Your LLC

Setting up the Structure of Your Entity

© SelfPublishingEmpire.com

Your brand-new LLC is kind of like a robot with an empty brain. It might look great from the outside, but it is otherwise mindless, with no instructions on how it should operate. You need to drop instructions into your brainless LLC so it knows what to do next, and how.

Initial Instructions

So far, the only instructions your LLC has come from the statutes of the state (in which it was formed) and its formation documents, called articles of organization.

Statutes

These rules dictate how the LLC will be set up, changed, who the partners are or could be, how it should remain active with your state, and when it can be put to death (dissolution or cancellation). But not much more.

Articles of Organization

Your formation documents don't shed much more light on how your LLC should be run. They only establish the name, who created the entity, who is the initial registered agent, and in some states, how the LLC is managed and who the initial managers/members are. Nothing more.

What's missing are instructions for how to operate, who is in charge, what ownership percentage the owners will take, and so many other issues.

Operating Agreement

The primary document which spells out how the LLC should be run is its operating agreement. This document could be as little as one page or as voluminous as hundreds of pages long. But it usually covers the following, in no specific order:

- Where are the corporate records kept?
- Who manages the LLC?
- Who are the owners (members)?
- What percentage ownership does each member have?
- What did each member give in cash (or equivalent) to the LLC to obtain their ownership percentage?
- Do they have meetings and if so when?
- What responsibilities do each of the managers/members have?
- How long will the LLC operate (i.e., # of years or some date in the future)?

The operating agreement may also spell out other issues, such as:

- When will there be a payout to the members?
- Do certain members receive a salary, and if so, how much and when?
- What if a manager/member dies prematurely?
- What if a manager/member wants to sell their interest?
- What if the LLC needs more capital?

In other words, like a partnership agreement, the operating agreement lays out all the details of how the LLC should be run and by whom.

A basic Operating Agreement is included with the purchase of this book. See how to download this in the "Forms" section of the Appendix.

Bank Resolution

Another common agreement, which is usually not part of the operating agreement, but still important, is a bank resolution. This spells out that the LLC wishes to have a bank account set up and which members/managers of the LLC will be in charge of it and have authority to write checks, set up credit accounts and so on. One of these resolutions is included, and download instructions are in the available in the "Forms" section of the Appendix.

You can move on to Chapter 3, Agreements and Contracts, and skip the next chapter, which is for corporations.

Ch IV. 2.

Next Steps For INCs

Setting up the Structure of Your Corporation

© SelfPublishingEmpire.com

(NOTE: If you don't have an actual Corporation, move on to the next chapter.)

You may think you're done once your corporation has been created, but this is only the starting point.

Unfortunately, a private corporation which is owned by even one person must follow the same rules as the billion-dollar public corporations do. That means setting up your corporation's structure.

Think of your corporation as having no brain, with no instructions on how it should be operated. You need to drop instructions into your brainless corporation, so it knows what to do next, and how.

Primary Instructions

Your corporation will get its primary marching orders from the state (in which it was formed) statutes. These rules dictate how the corporation will be owned, how it will be operated, who's in charge, what it must do to remain active with the state, how it can be changed, and when it can be put to death (dissolution).

Secondary Instructions

In addition to this are the corporation's bylaws, its secondary instructions. The bylaws are a private document, which lay out a few more specifics such as where the corporate records will be kept, when corporate meetings are handled and when, voting procedures, and so on.

Both sets of instructions essentially lay out how the corporation will be governed in its day-to-day affairs.

Who's in Charge?

Part of governing your corporation's affairs is determining who is in charge of your corporation, and what the roles are of each of the people involved in your corporation. The good news is Corporate Hierarchy is mostly the same within each for-profit corporation, regardless of state. Here's what it looks like:

Shareholders - These are the owners of the corporation and they are its foundation. Without them, the corporate pyramid would fall. Shareholders have votes on the biggest issues of the corporation:

- Electing and Firing Directors
- Its sale
- Its merger
- Changing stock structure

Directors - These folks are initially appointed/elected by the Incorporator (see below), and then after this they are elected (or fired) by the shareholders. The number of directors (can be one) and their responsibilities are limited by the corporation's bylaws and state's statutes. But in general, their job is to represent the shareholders in making sure the corporation is run correctly. Their functions/actions include:

- Electing, firing, and determining compensation of Officers
- Overall management of the corporation
- Taking on debt
- Taking issues to the shareholders
- Setting up special meetings
- Setting up the agendas for directors and shareholder meetings

Officers - These include the President, Secretary, Treasurer, and other primary officers of the corporation.

Other Parties Involved

There are other individuals who are involved in a corporation's operations, but who have limited responsibilities. These include:

The Incorporator - This is the person who creates the corporation by filing the articles of incorporation. After formation of the corporation, the incorporator has only one more function and then they are done forever: appointing/electing initial directors. This hand-over of responsibility is usually done in the articles of incorporation, but if the articles don't specify the "initial directors" by name, he/she/they must appoint or elect the initial directors. That can be done when the incorporator signs off on an appointment form naming the initial directors.

Registered Agent - This person has one simple responsibility: to be available for delivery of a lawsuit, or any other legal notice. Think of the agent as the primary legal contact for the corporation. When a notice or lawsuit or letter is delivered to the corporation's named registered agent, that corporation has been officially "served."

Each state sets the rules for the corporation's agent, but in general this person can be and usually is the principal of the entity (i.e., shareholder, director, or officer) or can be a designated third party (individual or entity) who is located at a physical address in the state of formation. The registered agent can be changed at any time to a person the officers of the corporation choose, and usually involves filing a notice of change with the Secretary of State of the formation state.

POST-FILING STEPS

You know all the players in your corporation and the rules

governing everyone; here are the tasks (Post Filing Steps) you must complete next.

> ⚠ **NOTE: You must do these BEFORE you can begin operating your corporation!**

Step I: Initial Organizational Meeting - This is the first "meeting" of the corporation, held by the corporation's newly appointed/elected initial director(s)--Yes, even if there's just one of you. This can be held immediately after the corporation has been formed, and if there is more than one director, it can be done in person or over the phone. Here's what you're going to do:

- Elect the corporate officers - This is the most important initial task: setting up the corporation's president, secretary and treasurer (can be the same person).
- Adopt bylaws - Remember these are the primary instructions.
- Bank resolution - Authorizing the corporation's representatives to open and manage a corporate bank account.
- Approve stock & seal - A corporation must issue stock and the type of stock certificate used must be approved first, along with a corporate seal (if any).
- Adopt a fiscal year - This is your corporate tax year, and usually ends December 31st.
- Direct reimbursement - The director(s) can direct the officers to reimburse you any of the expenses paid out by you personally to set up the corporation and get it running.
- Minutes of this meeting - This is your written proof that this meeting happened. Either these are expressed as corporate minutes or unanimous consent.

Step II: Issue Stock - Your corporation has directors and officers now, but it does not have an owner or owners. You may have started your corporation, but until your corporation issues stock to you, you are *not* an owner. Here's what you do:

- **Calculate # of pie pieces** - Like carving up a pie, a corporation's pie comes pre-carved into a certain number of pieces, called authorized shares. You can then dole out (i.e., issue) one or more pie pieces at a time, up to the maximum. Ownership is based on the total number of pieces you dole out: If two owners each get one piece (share), then each owns 50% of the total pie (even if there are more pieces (shares) left to issue.

- **Like a checkbook** - The stock certificates are like checks in a checkbook, where you list the total number of pieces (shares) a shareholder is going to get. Just fill in the name of the shareholder and the number of shares (usually as a number and written out like you do on a check). To start, use the first certificate in your book. If you don't have one, print one.

- **Sign & date** - The president and secretary sign and date the certificate, making it official.

- **Delivery** - Each certificate is issued to a shareholder who is buying that corporation's stock. That purchase can be done with a check (i.e., the amount needed to open a bank account), and for those funds given to the corporation in the form of "capital," the check-writer gets an issued stock certificate. The holder of that certificate is now an owner (AKA Stockholder) in the corporation.

Anything More?

Essentially, your structure is set. You'll have ongoing things (AKA Corporate Governance) that you will have to do throughout the year and each year, but that is a subject for another book (*Book#2 Entity Management*).

You can move on to Chapter 3, Agreements and Contracts.

Ch IV. 3.

Agreements & Contracts

If it's good enough for a traditional publisher...

If Amazon called you today and said, "We've decided that we want to run one of our operations out of your home, we don't want to pay you any money for this privilege, and we're going to do it on a handshake (i.e., we're not going draw up any sort of formal agreement)..." would you be good with that?

Of course you wouldn't! So why would you let YOU Publishing, LLC operate out of your home for free and with no formal agreement as well? Remember, YOU Publishing, LLC is a separate legal person. In other words, it is no different than Amazon or any other corporate entity... other than you happen to own it.

> ⚖️ **Arm's Length Transaction**
> There's a legal concept that says if two parties are acting in their own self-interests and independent of one another and they agree to something, it is usually concluded at the length of a handshake (or "arm's length"). That is, there is no insider dealing or special "under the table" deal made, and the agreement is usually codified in writing.

After you have formed your publishing entity, besides your operating agreement, there are three agreements you will want to secure between you and your author entity:

- **Copyright transfer agreements** - This formally moves the rights to your books, over to your entity.

- **Publishing agreement** - This formally hires YOU to write books for YOU Publishing, LLC (or YOU Publishing, INC.).

- **Bedroom lease agreement** - This is a lease agreement that allows YOU Publishing LLC to operate in your home.

Copyright transfer agreements

Whether you formally registered your books for federal copyright or not, YOU own the rights to your books (AKA copyright), because you wrote them. For YOU Publishing, LLC to gain formal rights to these books, and earn money by selling them, you must have a written agreement showing their transfer. Think of it as similar to transferring the deed to your home when you sell it.

You can find access to a template version of this agreement in the "Forms" section of the Appendix.

Publishing agreement

Even if you are a one-person operation, and your only intent is to write books, you must still have a contract. Would you write books for any traditional publisher without an agreement? Think of it another way: If it's good enough for a traditional publisher, why isn't it good enough for YOU Publishing?

You can find access to a template version of this agreement in the "Forms" section of the Appendix.

Bedroom lease agreement

This is also one more way you show separation between you (the author) and You Publishing LLC. You don't have to pay the same amount as you would for any lease, but you need to pay something from your entity to YOU for this right. How much is that worth: $50/month? $100? Whatever it is, just be sure you can pay it. Can you say, "EVICTION?" I'm just kidding. Also, keep in mind, you don't have to pay this every month. Payment can be made at the end of the year.

Like the other agreements, find access to a template version of this in the "Forms" section of the Appendix.

There is one final task to complete before you can officially begin operations of your Self-Publishing Empire™

Ch IV. 4.

Getting a Tax ID

YOU Publishing's Social Security Number

Ever notice how your SSN is used for everything, even though it was supposedly just to make sure you paid your Social Security taxes and later received your benefits?

Your author entity must get a similar number called an Employer ID Number or EIN. It was originally given to entities so that the IRS could make sure they properly tracked employees' tax withholdings. But just like your SSN is used for everything, so is your entity's EIN:

- Bank Account set-up

- All publishing platforms

- Vendor Account set-up

- Affiliate program sign-ups

How to get an EIN

Like SSNs, EINs are issued by the Social Security Administration and can be obtained in a matter of minutes online. Here's how:

1. Go here: https://sa.www4.irs.gov/modiein/individual/index.jsp

2. You'll be prompted to agree to their terms and conditions. Then just fill out the application.

3. At the end, after you've reviewed all the information you've typed in, you'll be asked whether you want your EIN mailed to your or generated immediately. Choose immediate. Make sure you can download PDF's. That is, your computer should have the ability to view, print and save PDF documents (i.e., via Adobe Reader).

   NOTE: Do NOT submit your application until you are sure you can download, print and save a PDF form. If you submit your application and you cannot retrieve your PDF approval letter from the IRS, you will NOT be able to get an approval letter from the IRS. EVER!

4. After you submit your form, immediately write down your EIN (or print that screen) before you download your IRS approval letter. This way, if something happens, you will at least have your EIN.

Future EIN changes

That approval letter has a tear-off mailer (for a standard window envelope). If you ever need to update the information you submitted to the IRS, or make some sort of change (i.e., the name of the company, or the responsible party, etc.), you can use this tear-off to mail the change request or form to the IRS. For more information on how to make changes to your entity's EIN, go here: http://www.smallbiz.com/Howto/notify-IRS-of-changes-to-EIN

YOU ARE DONE WITH YOUR FORMALITIES!

Are you ready to tell the world about your new author entity? It's time...

Ch V. Introducing YOU Publishing LLC

It's time to tell the world about your author entity

It is time to start telling the world about YOU Publishing LLC (or your corporation).

In other words, you will want to make sure that your author entity is the point-person for all things related to your Self-Publishing Empire™. This means, you will want all correspondence, income, book sales, contracts, vendor accounts, credit card transactions, and so on to essentially be made by your entity.

Here are some of the actions you will take in the next chapters.

1. **Setting Up Your Bank Accounts** - What bank to choose (you may want one besides your personal bank), what paperwork to bring with you, what to do if they don't like your paperwork, and so on.

2. **Credit Cards and Credit Lines** - I'll cover what you should do and what to avoid in this necessary step to grow your writing and publishing business.

3. **Registering With Publishing Platforms** - We'll dive into whether you should transfer your old accounts by making a few changes to reflect your new entity or set up new accounts altogether.

4. **Communications and Getting Social** - From this day forward, you'll need to decide who you really are when you correspond with others.

5. **Are YOU Done Yet** - What else lies ahead?

All right, let's draw back the curtains and show the world that you mean business!

Ch V. 1.

Setting Up Your Bank Accounts

What to say and do when you open an account

Just like you wouldn't want to mingle a relative's income and expenses with your personal checking account, you also don't want to mingle your corporate income and expenses with your personal account.

Remember, your author entity is a separate individual under the law, matriculated through the IRS with its own Social Security-like number (EIN). Likewise, it must have its own corporate checking account.

Having a corporate checking account in your name and the business name is not the same. If you set one up with you as the account holder, even if the business name is mentioned (i.e., a DBA), you're going to have to close this and set up a new corporate account. Your author entity must be the account holder of the corporate checking account, with only its officers or members/managers as the signor(s) on the account.

Remember, this separation from you as the individual owner of the business entity from the business entity itself is all important.

Setting Up Your Accounts

Before you set foot in your local bank branch (with corporate paperwork in hand), ready to open up a business checking account, there are a few things you'll need to consider.

Find a business bank

Most entrepreneurs open up their business accounts at the same place that they have their personal accounts. This actually makes sense from a banker's perspective because you already have a relationship (history) with that bank. And so it should be the first place you try. But prepare yourself, it may not be the last place you go.

You want a bank that is a partner to your business, preferably one that understands or knows your business (this part will be hard, but not impossible). You want a bank that wants to grow with you, to be with you all along the way. A business bank is one whose advertisements seem to target small businesses, and not just selling CDs to retirees or mortgages to newlyweds. In other words, who are your bank's target customers: regular individuals or businesses? One that targets primarily individuals is probably less in tune with the needs of your business.

You might be thinking, *Geez, I'm not making them a partner in my business. What difference does it make if I just want a checking account?* But a good bank can help your business as it grows along the way, assisting you in ways you can't even understand right now. Remember, you are not just an author writing books... You are the representative of a Self-Publishing Empire™.

So please take the time up front to find the right bank.

Types of accounts

Once you have identified your business bank, know that all banks offer multiple types of business checking accounts. Just remember, even the best bank is like any other product/service vendor who is trying to up-sell you to whatever product/service makes them the most money. Not every option they offer is necessary, nor the best for you and your business. So be prepared to be offered options when you go in. What's best for you? Well, that depends on what you're going to do. Here are a few considerations:

> Monthly Fees - Most banks offer a no monthly fee account, and most of the time that is what you should ask for. Sometimes banks have promotions for no-fee or some kind of other special account. Ask if they're running a promotion, or plan to run one soon. My bank does this a couple of times a year, even calling me to tell me about it. During promotions, bankers are eager to sign up as many new accounts as possible (because their managers look at their branch numbers).

> Checks - As a self-publisher, you will most likely never write a check, other than a few times per year, as most transactions (both incoming and outgoing) will be electronic. So the fees you pay for each check written are less important than a business that writes one hundred checks per month. Also, if there is a fee for basic checks (all you need), you might want to order basic starter checks from an outside vendor like Bradford Exchange (you can get them for under $20 delivered). Also remember that many banks offer electronic payments. Simply enter in a vendor's name and address, and when you receive a bill, direct the bank (online) to disburse a check to that vendor. Often there is no charge for this service.

> High Balance - Most banks will try to encourage you to maintain a high balance in your checking account, offering to

reduce or eliminate your account fees if you maintain that level. But don't just settle for this. Because commercial banks can't pay interest on checking accounts, it doesn't make sense to maintain a high balance. So find out what options they have on a minimum balance, no-fee, business checking account.

> Corporate Savings Account - Often there is a benefit to also opening a corporate savings account. You will need somewhere to park your SPE's vast revenues, so why not here? The interest rate is pretty meager, but there is a convenience to being able to transfer money back and forth between your business checking and savings accounts.

> Other Accounts - Some banks will give you credit for any other banking accounts you have with them: personal checking and/or savings, house mortgage, credit cards, etc. Find out if your prospective business bank does, as this can often affect the fees you pay (or don't pay).

Who should go with you (to the bank)
When you're ready to go to the bank and set up your account, consider who your account signors are. Most of the time your bank will require that ALL SIGNORS be present at the time of setting up the account. This of course may pose some significant barriers for you if your partner is located somewhere else, like a different state or country. If it's not possible for everyone to be there, you might have to make more than one visit, and/or schedule their coming in right after you. I have arranged for other signors to come into another branch to sign.

If every signor is not available at the time, you will want to discuss the options up front, so you don't waste a lot of your time.

NOTE: Because your SPE's legacy (passing on your SPE to your spouse and/or children) is important, you might want to make sure your spouse is one of the signors (and therefore an officer/member of your business entity) of your account. I will cover this more in *Author Legacy: Self-Publishing Empire™ Book #6.*

What to bring with you

Along with the signors, you will need to bring all your business entity's paperwork and a few other things. Here is what most banks will want to see:

For LLCs
- Articles of Organization (file stamped by the state)
- Initial Members/Managers - Something that names the initial members or managers (if they are not named on the Articles of Organization)
- Operating Agreement - Signed by all members/managers of the LLC
- Banking Resolution - Signed by all signors of the LLC

For Corporations
- Articles of Incorporation (file stamped by the state)
- Initial Directors - Something that names the initial directors (if they are not named on the Articles of Incorporation)
- Initial Organizational Meeting Minutes - Which show the election of the officers of the corporation
- Banking Resolution - Signed by all signors of the Corporation

ALSO, bring your Driver's License

NOTE: The above documents are what most banks would want, but your bank might ask for more or less than what is listed above. And that is because...

Bankers are stupid!

I mean this. Banks are built upon years of internal regulations and a legacy of an uber-conservative focus, all wrapped up in a book that tells their bankers what to do and how to do it. They don't think for themselves; they follow their rulebook.

I'm telling you this because often bankers will tell you something or demand something that either makes no sense or seems utterly ridiculous. If you don't experience this, consider yourself lucky. And understand that you can say, "No!"

I've personally helped hundreds of entrepreneurs set up their business accounts, often literally speaking to their bankers on the phone. And I've learned that sometimes you have to say, "No, that's not acceptable," followed by, "Let me talk to your manager."

The key is getting to someone who can make a decision, who can think through the illogic of their own banking rules and come up with a solution. Nine times out of ten, bringing a manager, even the branch manager, into the discussion will yield a solution. But if that doesn't work...

You can go elsewhere

If your prospective bank is making life difficult for your business when it comes to something as easy as setting up a business checking account, imagine how difficult they will make it when you ask for a credit card, or God-forbid if you want a credit line, or how about a merchant account? Some banks are just not the best banking partner for your self-publishing business. And that's okay. There are plenty of fish in the sea: Go elsewhere.

Remember I started this chapter with a list of items you should consider when looking for a business bank: one that is focused on finding solutions for your business and one who is a partner with your business, not an impediment. They are out there. So go find one.

More than one account

Personally, through different corporations and LLCs, I am a signor on multiple corporate checking accounts, corporate savings accounts, and uncountable vendor accounts. I tell you this not to brag, but to prepare you that you will probably open more than one corporate banking account. It is not a bad thing, assuming it helps you to achieve your goals.

Next, let's look at Credit Cards and Credit Lines.

Ch V. 2.

Credit Cards and Credit Lines

Whether to take the credit your bank will offer you

Just after you've formed your entity, you'll start to receive credit card offers in your Corporation or LLC's name. This is because credit card companies also recognize that entities are people too. I'm not going to get into a conversation about corporate credit, but let's just say that a corporation or LLC has its own credit (good or bad), aside from your own personal credit.

Likewise, because your Corporation is its own person, if it wishes to buy things on credit, it should use its own credit card.

Benefits (of a corporate credit card).

> Easier to claim deductions - When you use your corporate credit card for a purchase, you're very specifically segmenting your business purchases from your personal purchases (on your personal credit card). This makes it much easier to claim an expense is deductible: If you use your business credit card ONLY for

business, it makes your argument for deductibility much stronger.

> Build business credit - The longer your business entity has a credit card (and uses it), the stronger your business entity's credit file becomes. You may not care about credit for your business but having more is always helpful.

> Simpler accounting - When all of your business charges are on one statement, it makes it a lot easier to do your accounting.

> Other Bennies - frequent flyer miles, cash rewards, etc.

Where to Get One (a business credit card):

> Your bank - When I opened up an insurance agency thirty years ago, the president of a small business bank anchored in the same building came by and gave me a "Welcome" letter and said, "I set you up with a business credit card. If you want it, call this number." I've maintained an account with that bank ever since.

Today, banking is very different. But it still is beneficial to look at your business bank for a credit card as well. When you go to set up your business banking account, they will often offer this. Again, it may be very beneficial to do so. Just the convenience of paying off the balance via the connected business checking account is worth it.

> AMEX - My SPE has a business AMEX card. And there're many benefits to having one. Besides getting a cash rebate if I pay the balance early, it was easy to get. I believe AMEX is more open to offering businesses credit cards. But there are some negatives to an AMEX card:

> Fees - AMEX cards often have a higher annual fee. But when your renewal comes due, call AMEX and find out what they can do to assist you with this:

lower-fee card or special offer.

> Not taken everywhere - AMEX cards also charge the highest rate to merchants to process transactions, taking as much as 4% of every charge. Consequently, many merchants won't take AMEX cards at their stores.

> Go with the benefits - At every moment, there are different credit card companies, as well as vendors with their own exclusive cards, who offer special benefits to use their cards: frequent flyer miles, cash back, cruise ship credits, and much more. Be open to getting one.

> Personal Responsibility - Often cards issued to your business entity don't require a personal guarantee on your part. Not that this is an issue for you, but it's one of those benefits that's good to know.

Using Your Personal Card

If you just don't want to get a credit card for your Corporation or LLC, or maybe the benefit card you chose won't issue in your business entity's name. You can still use your own personal credit card and simply have your Corporation or LLC reimburse you for its use, making your expense its own. Just beware, you are opening yourself to questions if a personal charge "smells" more personal but is reimbursed by your author entity. So like anything else, your entity just needs to operate at "arm's length."

Other Borrowing Opportunities

Once your Corporation or LLC has developed its own credit, it can actually apply for business loans from your local bank.

But do not expect to be automatically loaned millions of dollars just because you have a corporation or LLC. Building credit for your SPE can sometimes be as difficult as building credit for you as a person.

It might take time.

Baby Steps

To build corporate credit you must take baby steps. Start with a secured credit card (if your bank won't issue a regular unsecured one), where you deposit a couple hundred dollars and the bank gives you credit for an equal amount. Continue to use, borrow, and pay off that secured credit card. At some point the bank will offer you an unsecured credit card. Take it! Once you've developed some history with your credit cards, other vendors and you have some income history (i.e., tax returns), your entity will be able to apply for bank loans and credit lines. This is not something you have to worry about now, but it is something to be aware of.

Beware

As I mentioned earlier, your author entity will receive many solicitations for credit. Most of them will not be legit or will be high-interest options you wouldn't want to take. Just file these in your circular file (after shredding).

Now it is time to update/set up your publishing platform accounts.

Ch V. 3.

Registering With Publishing Platforms

Now it's time to tell Amazon, et al.

Even if you have already set up a KDP account with Amazon or something similar with other publishing platforms, you are going to have to either change your existing account (that can be the easiest) or set up a new and separate account for your author entity. Remember, this is a new legal person and must have its own account.

Set Up New or Change Existing Account?

So which is better? That depends on what your goals are and what you have already published. For instance, if you have been self-publishing for years and have several titles in accounts spread out over multiple publishing platforms, setting up a new account for each and then transferring titles over to that new account would be a ginormous hassle.

On the other hand, if your new entity is a partnership and meant to be separate from your existing publishing entity (which might have accounts at different publishing platforms), then you will absolutely need to set up a different account for that entity. What about boxed-set partnerships or anthologies? You may still want to set up a different account, even if it's a one-and-done partnership. Consider these reasons:

- **Transparency** - You could even give a third party or one of your partners access to your account to verify all your numbers.
- **No questions** - Your partners will be less likely to ask questions about whether everything is above-board.
- **No commingling** - This is generally a no-no, even if everyone trusts everyone. It's just better to keep things separate.
- **No potential cross-liability** - If your new partnership inadvertently does something wrong (i.e., against Amazon's T.O.S.), there's less likelihood of it affecting the rest of your business.
- **Less risk against your partnership** - On the reverse, what if something happens to you personally, or to the rest of your business? If, for instance, a lien is placed on your own accounts, and your partnership was using the same account, all of its royalties would be attached as well.

Whether you are going to transfer/change your account or set up a new one, I have provided information about doing both below.

When to do this?

Before you start making changes to your publishing platform accounts or set up new accounts, the first question you will need to ask yourself is... When do I do this?

Because this is a tax question (more than a logistical one), the best person to pose this question to is your tax adviser. Keep in mind that when you do this (again, for tax purposes) you will be establishing an end date to your sole proprietorship (assuming you are already selling books before you formed your author entity) and a beginning date to the operations of your author entity (which is probably different than your entity's formation date). This means you will be operating in a split tax year, which means you will be essentially filing two tax returns (kind of), for two different "entities:"

- YOU will be doing business as YOU Publishing for tax year beginning 1/1 and ending on _X_ (the switch over date) &
- YOU Publishing LLC (or YOU Publishing, Inc.) for tax year beginning _X_ (the switch over date) and ending on 12/31.

"X" = the date you make the switch.

Logistical Suggestion: Although you will probably establish the first day of some month as the beginning date (for YOU Publishing, LLC's first tax year), you may want to make the transfer right after the 1st of the month. This will ensure that all deposits have most likely cleared Amazon, ACX and others by then.

All right, let's prepare for the switch-over, *before* you actually make the switch.

Amazon

Amazon Account Transfer

If you already have an account set up for you as an author, and your personal name is the account holder, showing the published books that you have already legally transferred (along with your other author business assets) over your new author entity, you can simply make changes to your existing account to complete the logistical "transfer" on Amazon.

Here's how:

1. Log into your KDP account (see the image at the start of this chapter) and click on the "Your Account" link at the very top right-middle side of the website.

2. In the Full Name field, enter in your author entity name instead of your personal name.

3. Update the Tax Information by clicking on the "View/Provide Tax Information" button and then taking the interview. Remember you are now speaking on behalf of your author entity (and not you the individual).

4. Finally, update the "Getting Paid" section with your new banking information. Be sure to remove the old bank information once the new information is added and verified.

5. That's it!

⚠ **Note**: Your personal Amazon account is probably directly connected to your KDP account. If you keep this, be sure others don't have access to it (i.e., your Prime account) and that any further business you conduct on Amazon is for your business, and not you personally. This will be vital during tax time. Also make sure everything connected to your existing Amazon and KDP account is business-specific (i.e., credit cards, etc.).

If you do this (change your Amazon account to business), you might then consider setting up a replacement personal account, with a different email address.

The Amazon TOS states that YOU cannot have more than one account. So two accounts with the same email address is impossible. Remember, we are talking two people here: YOU Publishing, LLC and YOU (the individual). For this reason, it is acceptable to have two *separate* Amazon accounts (one for each legal person).

Even if you have transferred your KDP account by changing your personal info to your author entity, there are reasons why you might want to set up a new KDP account.

Setting up a New KDP Account

When I set up a new publishing company with a partner, I needed to set up an entirely new account, separate from my own account (which was owned by my own author entity).

Here is the process I followed:

1. **Set up new email account** - I needed an email account which was different than the one I used for my author entity account. Luckily, we were already setting up a website and corresponding corporate emails. So this made everything easy for the next step. NOTE: To make it easy for our partnership, we set up a general email box (in addition to our individual corporate email accounts), and that general email address is what we used to set up our entity's Amazon accounts.

2. **Create a new Amazon membership** - Remember, it's a new legal person, which I want to keep separate from my other author entity account.

3. Now **set up the new KDP account**, using this new login.

4. Don't forget to **add your new tax and banking information**.

Other Platforms

If you are one of those self-published authors who sticks only to Amazon (I was), you're done and can move onto the next chapter. But for those of you who plan to publish or are already publishing in different formats (i.e. print, but not just KDP Print, audio, etc.) and publishing wide (on platforms outside of Amazon), your work has only just begun. I started with Amazon because they are the biggest and the easiest to work with (for what we're doing here).

But don't forget these platforms too:

- **ACX** - Yes, it is part of Amazon, but operated separately. From what I can see, you should be able to simply make changes to your existing account by updating the Personal Information, Tax Information and Bank Information.

- **Ingram** – These wonderful folks will help you make the change.

- **Others** - I haven't yet experimented with changes to the other platforms out there, but I'd wager their processes are similar to Amazon. Most likely you will need to work with their customer service departments to make final changes. I list the biggest, so you don't forget them:
    - B&N
    - Google
    - Apple
    - Kobo

Other Vendors

I am making a note here, rather than giving you an uber-short separate chapter. Just like your relationships with publishing platforms, you will also need to make changes to any other vendor accounts you already had set up personally but plan to continue doing business with through your new author entity. Again, you will probably have the option of either changing the information in your existing account or setting up a new account.

Using Personal Accounts In Your Business
This is something I plan to cover in the final book of the series:
But it bears mention here.

You do NOT have to change <u>every</u> account you have to your entity: change only those where it makes sense to do so. If you do wish to use a personal account for your business, just do it as any employee would do it for any employer.

For instance, if you prefer to use a mileage credit card to purchase seats on an airline (also via your personal account), just be sure that you submit a reimbursement request from you to your author entity. This is how your personal expense is made into a business expense (assuming there is a legitimate reason for doing this). And it avoids the complication of trying to switch a personal account (i.e., your mileage credit card) to business, which might not even be possible.

Below, I give you a few examples of potential vendors to jog your memory, so that you don't forget someone:

- Amazon Central - Do NOT forget this.
- Audible - Do you listen to audiobooks for fun? Since you are going to want to sell books here, make future listening a business expense and set up an account in your business name.
- BookBub & Other Promo Newsletters - None of these necessarily have to be changed.
- Advertising sites - FB, BookBub, AMS should at a minimum have your business credit card there.
- Other suppliers of products that you use as research for your books
- Web hosting company

Okay, let's talk about how you communicate with others from now on.

Ch V. 4.

Communications & Getting Social

Who's talking now?

You have a dilemma ahead of you... How are you going to identify yourself?

What I'm asking you to consider is are you corresponding/communicating with people as YOU the author or YOU the Manager (or Member-Manager) of YOU Publishing, LLC?

This is very important, because how you communicate with the outside world will determine whether it looks at you as an individual or as a representative of your author entity. Remember, your entity is separate from you, so all of your communications (on behalf of your entity) should represent this.

Think of it this way: If you were going to send an email to someone on behalf of your brother, would you use your information or your brother's information, or would you simply say that it is YOU, on behalf of your brother?

It is similar for your author entity.

In a nutshell, when you're sending out communication, signing an agreement, posting on Facebook, etc., who is the communication coming from: you the author or you the representative of your author entity?

If it is coming from the company, be sure it is obvious, and where your name is mentioned, add "Member" or President" (or whatever your official title is). Setting up an official FB page, website and email, and printing business cards all helps to cement your relationship to the entity.

That way, when you post on FB or send your emails as an author, there won't be any confusion. People will know they are dealing with your Self-Publishing Empire™.

Ch V. 5.

Are YOU Done Yet?

You have completed a HUGE first step!

Fantastic job!

Congratulations!

You have just taken a giant first step in creating your Self-Publishing Empire™. But our journey does not end here. Check out What Comes Next...

What Comes Next?

What to expect in subsequent *Self-Publishing Empire™* books

Thank you for reading!

Please take a quick moment and rate this book on Amazon and Goodreads.

Want to see changes?
If you want to see any changes, including any additions, more detail or less detail on any subject, or removal of anything, or if you just see something you're sure is wrong, please tell me directly. Email me at michael@mlbanner.com and let me know.

Okay, now what?

Appendix
At the back of this book is an Appendix, with the following:

- **State Agency Info** - A 51-state rundown of each state's agencies (remember, DC is included) that you'll have to deal with to form and run your entity. Find your state of choice and visit the sites listed and/or contact information.

- **Forms** - The minimum documents you will need to set up and initially maintain your LLC or corporation.

- **Free Incorporation Coupon** - Get your entity formed for free; you just pay the state fees. Simply use the coupon number in this coupon.

The *Self-Publishing Empire*™ Series
And there's much more to come...

As I mentioned earlier, because I couldn't fit all I wanted into one book, and I wanted to get this book out there as soon as possible, I'll be releasing other books in the series over the coming months. Here is a list of what else to expect in the Series (title names may change slightly):

Book #2: MANAGING YOUR ENTITY
In Book #2, we'll dive into the details about managing your self-publishing entity to make sure it's compliant with the IRS, your state, and your local municipalities (you may have more than one). Specifically, we'll look at:

1. Required Internal Actions & Documentation
2. LLC Management
3. INC Management
4. Licensing
5. What to Do with the State
6. What to Do with the IRS
7. Handling Payroll and Other Ongoing Logistics
8. Making Changes
9. Other Compliance Red Fags
10. Closing Down an Entity
11. Transferring an Entity

Book #3: PROTECTING YOUR INTELLECTUAL PROPERTY
In Book #3, we'll cover the often-misunderstood subject of IP, or intellectual property. We'll discuss some effective techniques for you to easily and inexpensively protect your books, covers, and

titles, as well as why this is so important. Here are some of the subjects we'll dive into:

1. What are Your Empire's Brands?
2. How Do You Protect Them?
3. Copyright Protection
4. Amazon Just Took Down My Books For Trademark Infringement
5. Cockygate Revisited
6. Why Authors Need to Trademark, and How
7. Other Defenses that Work and Don't
8. Vigorous Defense of Your IP

Book #4: MULTIPLE STREAMS OF INCOME

In Book #4, we'll talk about some ways other SPE authors have leveraged their assets to generate multiple streams of income which you can perpetuate, long after you've published a book. Here are just a few:

1. Become a Hybrid
2. Put Your Books on Autopilot
3. More Formats
4. Co-Author/Partner
5. Box Sets - New ideas
6. Affiliate Revenues (Amazon & Others)
7. SWAG for Sale
8. Podcasts
9. Becoming a Publisher of Other Authors' Books
10. License Your World
11. More...

Book #5: CO-AUTHORING/PARTNERING

In Book #5, we'll cover in detail the subject of co-authoring. Besides just co-writing a book or series with another author, we'll offer many real-life examples as we discuss the details:

1. Questions You and Your "Partner" Should Ask Each Other
2. Defining Roles
3. How to Divide the Income
4. The Business Side of Things - Whose Account or a New One; Which Bank
5. Writing Agreements
6. Setting Up Separate LLCs for Each Partnership
7. How to Do the Contracts

Book #6: Author Legacy

Book #6 tackles the difficult subject of planning for your family after you are gone. And by planning for the "what-ifs," you'll end up making the management of your self-publishing empire far more efficient. Whether you're young or old, this taboo subject is absolutely crucial.

1. Why This is Important
2. Review of What's Been Done (Which Helps Your Legacy Planning)
3. Plan for Succession
4. The Joys of Family Partnerships
5. Taking Inventory
6. How to Communicate That and to Whom
7. Next Steps Now

Bonus Section - ADVANCED TECHNIQUES

1. Income Splitting
2. Separate Ownership of Each Book/Series
3. Other Ideas

Book #7: What You Need To Know About Taxes

What's better than lowering your taxes? In Book #7, we'll cover not only the basics, but also some of the more complicated methods of lowering your SPE's tax bill. Here's an overview:

1. Tax Basics for Businesses
2. Author Income and Why It's Different
3. Self-Employment Taxes & S-Corps
4. The Tax Cuts and Jobs Act
5. Reporting to the IRS & Your State
6. The Power of an Accountant/CPA
7. Year-End Stuff

Bonus Section - WRITE OFF YOUR NEXT VACATION
(Yep, this is the fun stuff)

1. Making Your Vacation Tax-Free
2. Why Not Do Research on that Vacation
3. Writers' Conferences
4. Prime & KU Subscriptions
5. Other Books

About The Author
(When he's not writing business books)

Michael "ML" Banner is an award winning &
international best-selling author of apocalyptic thrillers.

Six of his books were #1 Amazon best-sellers in one or more
genres. He's won two Readers Favorite Medals for different genres: a
silver for *MADNESS* in 2018 in Horror and a gold for *Highway* in 2016 in
Thrillers. His work is both traditionally published and self-published.

Often his thrillers are set in far-flung places, as Michael uses his
experiences from visiting dozens of countries--some multiple times--over
the years (and all tax free). His last two transatlantic cruises were the
foreground of *The Final Outbreak*.

A serial entrepreneur, having formed multiple businesses over
the years, he founded and still runs SmallBiZ.com, which helps small
businesses create and maintain entities, forming almost 100,000 entities
over its 20 years of existence.

Most recently, Michael and another author friend (Jay Falconer)
created and co-manage Mission Critical Publishing, LLC. Authors are

offered the opportunity to write within one or more worlds and, using methods they've developed over the years, along with thousands of avid followers, launch new series into best-selling categories otherwise difficult for authors to do on their own. Michael and Jay are working with several authors currently, co-writing dozens of books which they expect to launch in the coming months.

When not running a business or writing his next book, you might find Michael hunting, traveling abroad, or reading a Kindle with his toes in the water (name of his personal publishing company) in the Sea of Cortez (Mexico). That's because he and his wife split time between the deserts of Arizona and the beaches of Mexico.

Connect With Michael L. Banner

Tell me about your own Self-Publishing Empire – I would love to hear from you!

Email: michael@mlbanner.com

For My NonFiction
Website: http://selfpublishingempire.com
Facebook: facebook.com/selfpubempire

For My Fiction
Website: http://mlbanner.com
Facebook: facebook.com/authormlbanner
Twitter: @ml_banner

Appendix

Here are some additional resources for your SPE

1. State Agencies & Websites: Formations, Licensing & Revenue
2. Forms
3. Free Incorporation Coupon

State Agencies & Websites

The following state agencies are in charge of LLC and corporation filings. There contact phone numbers are provided (to answer any questions), a link to check name availability in that state, and the links to either filing online or download the appropriate forms and instructions for filing.

ALABAMA
Alabama Secretary of State
(334) 242-5324

Name Check:

http://arc-sos.state.al.us/CGI/CORPNAME.MBR/INPUT

Online Filing of LLCs:

https://www.sos.alabama.gov/business-entities/llcs

Online Filing of Corporations:

https://www.sos.alabama.gov/business-entities/domestic-corporations

ALASKA
Division Corps, Business and Professional Licensing (CBPL)
907-465-6448

Name Check:

http://commerce.alaska.gov/CBP/Main/CBPLSearch.aspx?mode=Corp

Online Filing of LLCs:

https://www.commerce.state.ak.us/CBP/Corporation/startpage.aspx?file=CRFIL&entity=LLCO&isforeign=N

Online Filing of Corporations:

https://www.commerce.alaska.gov/CBP/Corporation/startpage.aspx?file=CRFIL&entity=BUSC&isforeign=N

ARIZONA
Arizona Corporation Commission
(602) 542-3026

Name Check:

https://ecorp.azcc.gov/EntitySearch/Index

Online Filing of INCs & LLCs

https://ecorp.azcc.gov/AzAccount?sessionExpired=False
Note: you'll create an account first.

ARKANSA
Arkansas Secretary of State
(501) 682-3409 or 888-233-0325

Name Check:

http://www.sosweb.state.ar.us/corps/search_all.php

Online Filing of INCs & LLCs:

https://www.ark.org/sos/ofs/docs/index.php

CALIFORNIA
California Secretary of State
(916) 657-5448 -Corp #2, LLC #3

Name Check:

https://businesssearch.sos.ca.gov/

Online Filing of LLCs:

http://www.sos.ca.gov/business-programs/bizfile/

Filing of INCs:

https://www.sos.ca.gov/business-programs/business-entities/forms/
(by paper form)

COLORADO
CO Secretary of State
(303)-894-2200 #2, #3 (#0 – staff member)

Name Check:

http://www.sos.state.co.us/biz/BusinessEntityCriteriaExt.do

Online Filing of INCs & LLCs:

http://www.sos.state.co.us/pubs/business/main.htm

CONNECTICUT
Connecticut Secretary of State
(860) 509-6003; #2 Questions

Name Check:

http://www.concord-sots.ct.gov/CONCORD/online?sn=PublicInquiry&eid=9740

Online Filing of INCs & LLCs:

https://www.concord-sots.ct.gov/CONCORD/customer?eid=9799

DELAWARE
Division of Corporations
(302) 739-3073 #0

Name Check:

https://icis.corp.delaware.gov/Ecorp/EntitySearch/NameSearch.aspx

Filing of INCs & LLCs:

https://corp.delaware.gov/corpforms/
(Paper filings only)

DISTRICT OF COLUMBIA (DC)
DCRA Business Regulation Administration
(202) 442-4432 Filing #2, 0

Name Check:

https://corponline.dcra.dc.gov/Account.aspx/LogOn?ReturnUrl=%2f

Online Filing of INCs & LLCs:

https://corponline.dcra.dc.gov/Account.aspx/LogOn?ReturnUrl=%2f

FLORIDA
Department of State
(850) 245-6052 #0

Name Check:

http://www.sunbiz.org/search.html

Online Filing of INCs & LLCs:

https://efile.sunbiz.org/onlmenu.html

GEORGIA
Secretary of State
(404) 656-2817 #1, then #4

Name Check:

https://ecorp.sos.ga.gov/BusinessSearch

Online Filing of INCs & LLCs:

https://ecorp.sos.ga.gov/Account

HAWAII
Department of Commerce and Consumer Affairs
Name Check:

http://www.ehawaiigov.org/dcca/bizsearch/exe/bizsearch.cgi

Online Filing of INCs & LLCs:

https://hbe.ehawaii.gov/BizEx/filing/expert/index.eb

IDAHO
Idaho Secretary of State
(208) 334-2301

Name Check:

https://sosbiz.idaho.gov/search/business

Online Filing of LLCs:

https://sosbiz.idaho.gov/auth?from=/queue/business

ILLINOIS
Secretary of State, Business Services
(217) 782-9520 LLC #1,#1, Corp #3

Name Check:

https://www.ilsos.gov/corporatellc/

Online Filing of INCs & LLCs:

http://www.cyberdriveillinois.com/services/business.html

INDIANA
Secretary of State
(317) 232-6576

Name Check:

https://bsd.sos.in.gov/publicbusinesssearch

Online Filing of INCs & LLCs:

https://inbiz.in.gov/start-business/step-one/

IOWA
Secretary of State
(515) 281-5204

Name Check:

https://sos.iowa.gov/search/business/(S(1lvzb2bxl4dawh55so4su445))/

search.aspx

Online Filing of INCs & LLCs:

https://filings.sos.iowa.gov/Account/Login

KANSAS
Secretary of State
(785) 296-4564

Name Check:

https://www.accesskansas.org/bess/flow/main?execution=e2s1

Online Filing of INCs & LLCs:

http://www.kssos.org/business/business.html

KENTUCKY
Secretary of State
(502) 564-3490 – Filings (8:00 – 4:30)

Name Check:

http://app.sos.ky.gov/ftsearch/

Online Filing of INCs & LLCs:

https://secure.kentucky.gov/sos/ftbr/RegistrationHome.aspx

LOUISIANA
Corporations Division
(225) 925-4704

Name Check:

http://www.sos.la.gov/BusinessServices/SearchForLouisianaBusinessFili

ngs/Pages/default.aspx

Online Filing of INCs & LLCs:

http://www.sos.la.gov/BusinessServices/FileBusinessDocuments/Pages/

default.aspx

MAINE
Secretary of State
(207) 624-7752 – hold for general info

Name Check:

http://icrs.informe.org/nei-sos-icrs/ICRS?MainPage=x

Online Filing of INCs & LLCs:

http://www.maine.gov/sos/cec/corp/index.html

MARYLAND
Department of Assessments and Taxation
(410) 767-1350 # 1

Name Check:

https://egov.maryland.gov/BusinessExpress/EntitySearch

Online Filing of INCs & LLCs:

http://www.maryland.gov/pages/business.aspx

https://egov.maryland.gov/businessexpress for expedited filings

MASSACHUSETTS
The Commonwealth of Massachusetts
(617) 727-9640

Name Check:

http://corp.sec.state.ma.us/corpweb/corpsearch/CorpSearch.aspx

Online Filing of INCS & LLCs:

https://corp.sec.state.ma.us/corp/loginsystem/login_form.asp?FilingMethod=I

MICHIGAN
Dept. of Licensing and Regulatory Affairs
(517) 241-6470

Name Check:

https://cofs.lara.state.mi.us/corpweb/CorpSearch/CorpSearch.aspx

Online Filing of INCs & LLCs:

https://cofs.lara.state.mi.us/corpweb/LoginSystem/ExternalLogin.aspx

MINNISOTA
Secretary Of State
(651)296-2803 #2, #1 name availability #2 business entities

Name Check:

https://mblsportal.sos.state.mn.us/Business/Search

Online Filing of INCs & LLCs:

http://mblsportal.sos.state.mn.us/

MISSISSIPPI
Secretary Of State
(601) 359-1350 Ask for Business Services

Name Check:

https://corp.sos.ms.gov/corp/portal/c/page/corpBusinessIdSearch/port

al.aspx?#clear=1

Online Filing of INCs & LLCs:

http://www.sos.ms.gov/BusinessServices/Pages/default.aspx

MISSOURI
Secretary of State
(573) 751-4153 or (866) 223-6535 Filing #2

Name Check:

https://www.sos.mo.gov/BusinessEntity/soskb/csearch.asp

Online Filing of INCs & LLCs:

https://bsd.sos.mo.gov/loginwelcome.aspx?lobID=1

MONTANA
Secretary of State
(406) 444-3665

Name Check:

https://app.mt.gov/bes/

Online Filing of INCs & LLCs:

https://app.mt.gov/epass-idp/Authn/EpassLogin/

NEBRASKA
Secretary of State
(402) 471-4079

Name Check:

https://www.nebraska.gov/sos/corp/corpsearch.cgi?nav=search

Online Filing of INCs & LLCs:

http://www.sos.ne.gov/business/corp_serv/index.html

NEVADA
Secretary of State
(775) 684-5708 #2

Name Check:

https://esos.nv.gov/EntitySearch/OnlineEntitySearch

Online Filing of INCs & LLCs:

https://www.nvsilverflume.gov/home

NEW HAMPSHIRE
Secretary of State
(603) 271-3244 #0

Name Check:

https://quickstart.sos.nh.gov/online/BusinessInquire

Online Filing of INCs & LLCs:

https://quickstart.sos.nh.gov/online/Account

NEW JERSEY
Corporation Filing Unit
(609) 292-9292 #1

Name Check:

https://www.njportal.com/DOR/BusinessNameSearch/Search/Availability

Online Filing of INCs & LLCs:

https://www.njportal.com/DOR/BusinessFormation/CompanyInformati

on/BusinessName

NEW MEXICO
Secretary of State
(505) 827-4508 #2, #1, #1

Name Check:

https://portal.sos.state.nm.us/BFS/online/CorporationBusinessSearch

Online Filing of LLCs:

https://portal.sos.state.nm.us/BFS/online/Account

NEW YORK
Department of State
(518) 473-2492

Name Check & Online Filing of INCs & LLCs:

https://appext20.dos.ny.gov/ecorp_public/f?p=2020:1:0::NO:::

After conducting name search start online filing

NORTH CAROLINA
Secretary Of State
(919) 814-5400, #1, #3

Name Check:

https://www.sosnc.gov/search/index/corp

Online Filing of INCs & LLCs:

https://www.sosnc.gov/divisions/business_registration/online_business

_services

NORTH DAKOTA
State of North Dakota
(701) 328-4284

Name Check:

https://secure.apps.state.nd.us/sc/busnsrch/busnSearch.htm

Online Filing of INCs & LLCs:

https://firststop.sos.nd.gov/forms/new/523

OHIO
Secretary of State
(614) 466-3910 or (877) 767-3453 #1

Name Check:

https://businesssearch.sos.state.oh.us/?=businessDetails

Online Filing of INCs & LLCs:

https://bsportal.sos.state.oh.us/(S(cxjdw1di2exqypiidl5vy4zg))/Login.as

px

OKLAHOMA
Secretary of State
(405) 522-2520

Name Check:

https://www.sos.ok.gov/cart/contact.aspx?ReturnUrl=/cart/work.aspx?

f=366

Online Filing of INCs & LLCs:

https://www.sos.ok.gov/corp/filing.aspx

OREGON
Secretary of State
(503) 986-2200 #2

Name Check:

http://egov.sos.state.or.us/br/pkg_web_name_srch_inq.login

Online Filing of INCs & LLCs:

https://secure.sos.state.or.us/cbrmanager/index#stay

PENNSYLVANIA
Pennsylvania Department of State
(717) 787-1057 #5

Name Check:

https://www.corporations.pa.gov/search/corpsearch

Online Filing of INCs & LLCs:

https://www.corporations.pa.gov/Account/ValidateUser

RHODE ISLAND
Office of the Secretary of State
(401) 222-3040

Name Check:

http://ucc.state.ri.us/CorpSearch/CorpSearchInput.asp

Online Filing of LLCs:

http://ucc.state.ri.us/loginsystem/login_form.asp

SOUTH CAROLINA
Secretary of State
(803) 734-2158, #1

Name Check:

https://businessfilings.sc.gov/BusinessFiling/Entity/Search

Online Filing of INCs & LLCs:

https://sos.sc.gov/online-filings/business-entities/file-and-search-online

SOUTH DAKOTA
Secretary of State
(605) 773-4845

Name Check:
http://sdsos.gov/business/search.aspx
Online Filing of INCs & LLCs:
https://sosenterprise.sd.gov/BusinessServices/Business/RegistrationInst
r.aspx

TENNESSEE
Secretary of State
(615) 741-2286

Name Check:

http://www.tennesseeanytime.org/sosname/

Online Filing of INCs & LLCs:
https://tnbear.tn.gov/Ecommerce/RegistrationType.aspx

TEXAS
Secretary of State
(512) 463-5555
Name Check:
Call (512) 463-5555
Online Filing of LLCs:
https://direct.sos.state.tx.us/acct/acct-login.asp

UTAH
State of Utah
(801) 530-6311

Name Check:

https://secure.utah.gov/bes/

Online Filing of INCs & LLCs:

http://www.commerce.utah.gov/cor/

VERMONT
Corporations Division
(802) 828-2386, #0

Name Check:

https://www.vtsosonline.com/online/BusinessInquire/

Online Filing of INCs & LLCs:

https://www.vtsosonline.com/online

VIRGINIA
Virginia State Corporation Commission
(804) 371-9733 #1

Name Check:

https://sccefile.scc.virginia.gov/NameAvailability

Online Filing of INCs & LLCs:

https://sccefile.scc.virginia.gov/

WASHINGTON
Secretary Of State
(360) 725-0377, #0

Name Check:

https://www.sos.wa.gov/corps/

Online Filing of LLCs:

http://www.sos.wa.gov/corps/ProfitCorporationsOnlineandPaperRegist

ration.aspx

Online Filing of INCs:

https://corps2.sos.wa.gov/Profit/Pages/StartPage.aspx

WEST VIRGINIA
Corporations Division
(304) 558-8000

Name Check:

http://www.wvsos.com/wvcorporations/

Online Filing of INCs & LLCs:

http://www.wvsos.com/common/startbusiness.htm

WISCONSIN
Department of Financial Institutions
(608) 261-7577 (option #5)

Name Check:

http://www.wdfi.org/corporations/crispix/

Online Filing of INCs & LLCs:

https://www.wdfi.org/apps/CorpFormation/

WYOMING
Secretary of State
(307) 777-7311 or 7312

Name Check:

https://wyobiz.wy.gov/Business/FilingSearch.aspx

Online Filing of INCs & LLCs:

https://wyobiz.wy.gov/Business/RegistrationType.aspx

Forms

Rather than provide an agreement example or the text of an agreement here (which would be hard to use from a paperback, and harder to use from an eBook), I've set up an agreement repository at SelfPublishingEmpire.com. And you will have access to it for free!

Here are the agreements I'll supply because you have purchased this book:
- LLC Worksheet
- INC Worksheet
- Operating Agreement (Basic)
- Bank Resolution
- Copyright Transfer Agreement
- Publishing Agreement
- Bedroom Lease Agreement
- More – I will add others later

Each agreement can be downloaded, filled in on your computer, printed and ready for signature.

How to access:
1. Go to http://selfpublishingempire.com/forms and enter in your name and email address;
2. Watch your email for verification and then you'll be sent a password;
3. Go to SelfPublishingEmpire.com/forms and enter your password.

Free Incorporation Coupon

As a purchaser of this book, SmallBiZ.com will set up one INC or LLC for you for free. In other words, SmallBiZ.com will waive its normally low $25 fee to form your Self-Publishing Empire™ (either as an INC or LLC) just for you. You'll pay only your state's filing fees (as little as $50, depending on the state in which you reside or want to form in) and a small shipping and handling fee ($6 for Standard Shipping).

Here's how to take advantage of this deal:

1. Go to SmallBiZ.com's Quick Quote area on their website: https://secure.smallbiz.com/incorporator/quickquote1what.cfm

2. Get a quote for either Form an LLC or Incorporate.

3. At the end of the form enter in the Promotional Code "SPE 2019" and click the Apply button. The $25 will be removed from your order.

4. After you submit, SmallBiZ.com will ask where you got this code. Just say, "I purchased ENTITY SET UP by Michael L. Banner" and the discount will be approved.

Made in the USA
Middletown, DE
03 January 2023

21132408R00119